PICTURING JOY

PICTURING JOY
STORIES OF CONNECTION

GEORGE LANGE

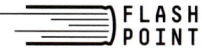

FLASH POINT

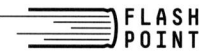

Published by Flashpoint™ Books, Seattle
www.flashpointbooks.com
Produced by Indelible Editions

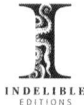

INDELIBLE
EDITIONS

Design: Andrea Duarte, Indelible Editions
ISBN (hardcover): 978-1-959411-35-2
ISBN (ebook): 978-1-959411-36-9

Library of Congress Control Number: 2023909816

First Edition

Printed in China

TO EVERYONE WHO HAS OPENED
A DOOR AND INVITED ME IN

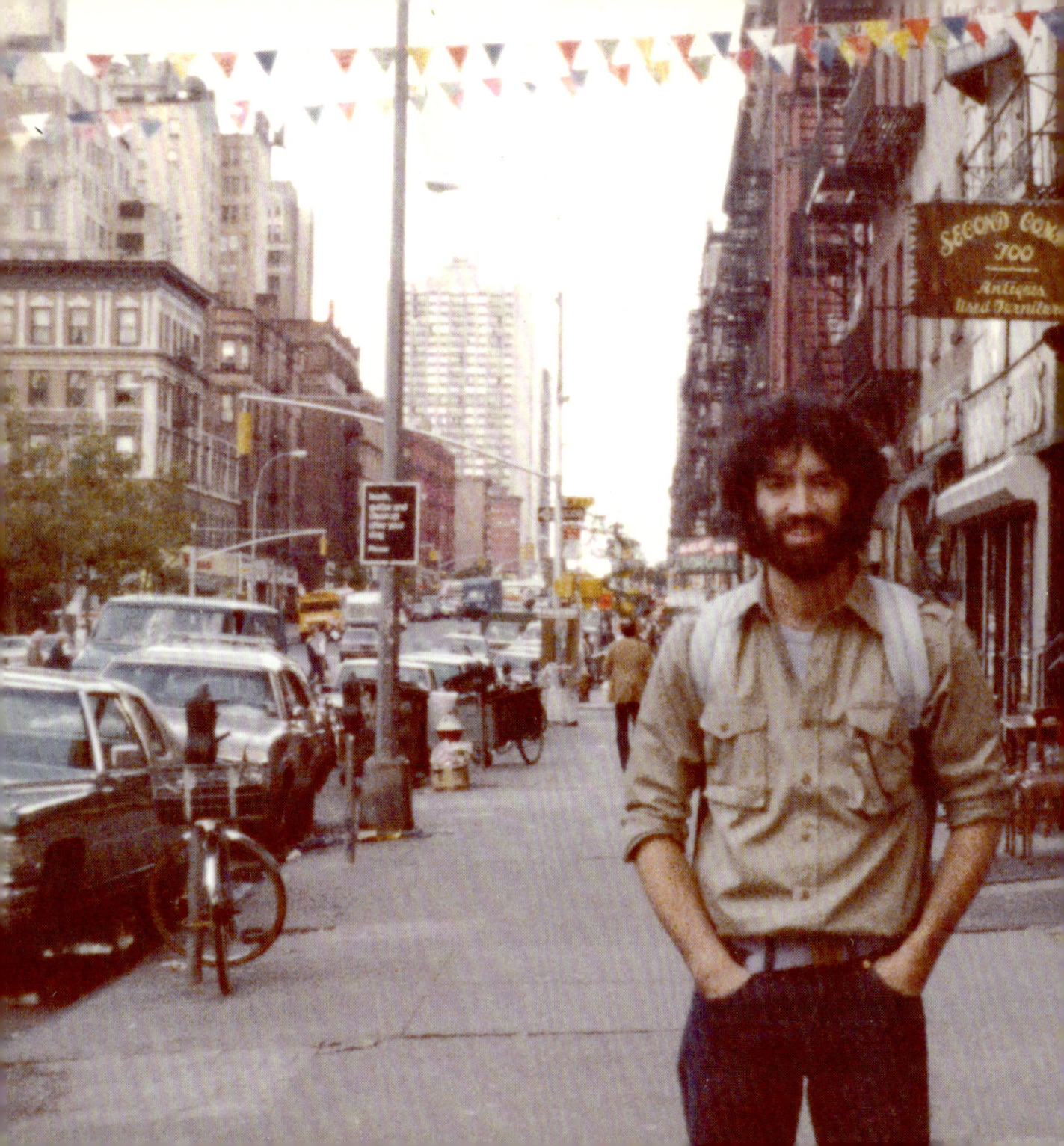

INTRODUCTION

When applying to the Rhode Island School of Design, my classmate Liza wrote, "Asking me why I want to come to RISD is like asking a clown why they want to join the circus." That was her entire essay and they accepted her. My essay was a little longer, but the sentiment was the same. RISD was where I belonged.

The spring before I started, I knew nothing about art school, but I knew I wanted to be a photographer. I rented a room for the night above a really loud night club off of Benefit Street in Providence and took a tour of the college. When we came through the student union and out onto Benefit Street, the tour guide pointed to Benson Hall, across the street where the photo department was housed. I looked up at it, thinking, "This is where I will be studying photography in the fall."

I went back to my little room, its walls pulsating from the nightclub below, and filled out the application. I have no idea why they accepted me. My drawings were horrible. My photography was definitely not "art" as they defined it. But I had the great desire, and maybe that came through.

Unlike the cerebral photography of my classmates, my photos were more about this feeling of joy I was trying to capture. They weren't carefree and silly, but they were also not that serious. Searching for joy doesn't mean you are happy all the time. Joy can be a goal. Joy can be born out of sadness. Joy is in your DNA, even if it feels out of reach. And sometimes, joy can allow you to feel time stand still.

Joy is not something art students like to discuss, so I just wove it into my work. It made me an outsider, but I didn't know how to be anyone besides who

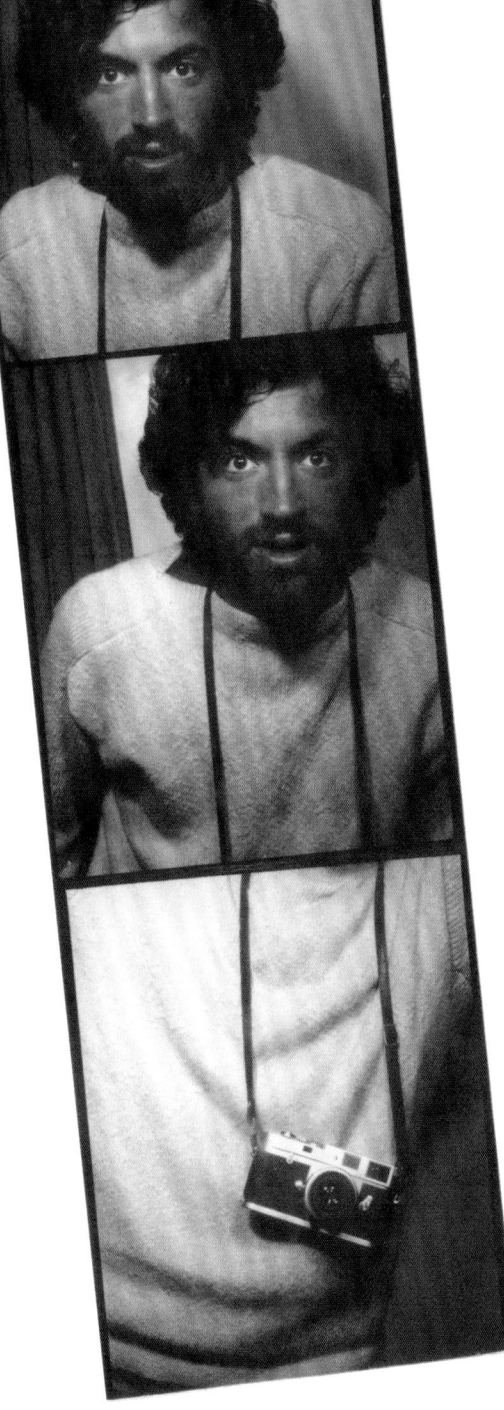

I was. To me, my work was never precious. I never longed for it to be hung in a museum. Truthfully, I wasn't even that into photography as a medium. I just loved taking pictures.

As a professional photographer, you spend less than 10 percent of your time behind the camera—a fact that I hate but is true. The photos are what you get to share with the world. They are the artifacts of the experience that you create. At RISD, the goal was to create photographs that were art. In my career, I've made an art out of creating experiences that I get to photograph. People are always surprised when I say I don't care that much about what something looks like. I want my photos to reflect what I feel more than what I see.

Some of the photos in this book were taken recently and some very early in my career. I love how they all get to hang out together in these pages. Strangers and friends have given me gifts my entire life, including their time and enthusiasm. But mostly what they have given me is themselves. My mission has been to share those gifts through my photographs. It is kind of like a parade I started when I was very young of people I have photographed, and continue adding to today. The thread that runs through all of my photos is the joy at the center of my life.

In *Picturing Joy*, I'm sharing stories of how I captured these moments. I hope it helps you notice and cherish them in your own life.

At our weekly critiques at RISD, my teacher always saved
me for last. My work was a whole thing: Sound. Projections.
Music. Freshly squeezed orange juice. All week long I would
take my photographs and record conversations, then I'd stay
up for twenty-four hours putting it all together like a big
collage. I edited together conversations people would have
with me but never with each other. I illustrated the audio with
hundreds of photos that were also like conversations. I shot
sequences when a single photo would not work. When my
presentation was done, no one would say anything at first.
Then, my professor Wendy Snyder MacNeil would yell out,
"Go, George, GO!" Wendy had a mantra she would tell me
every week at the end of class: "Don't think! Just take
pictures." I knew how to do that.

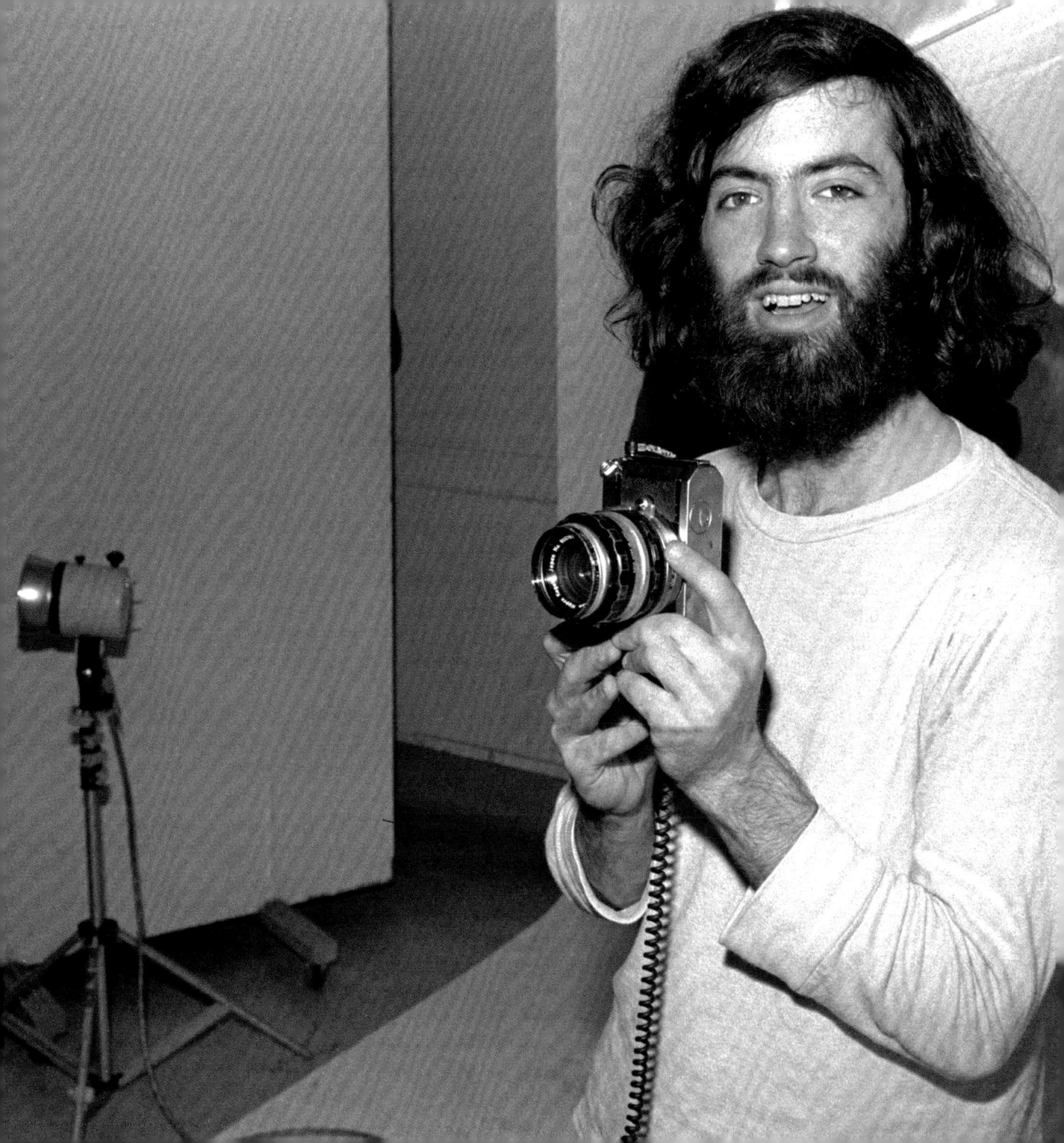

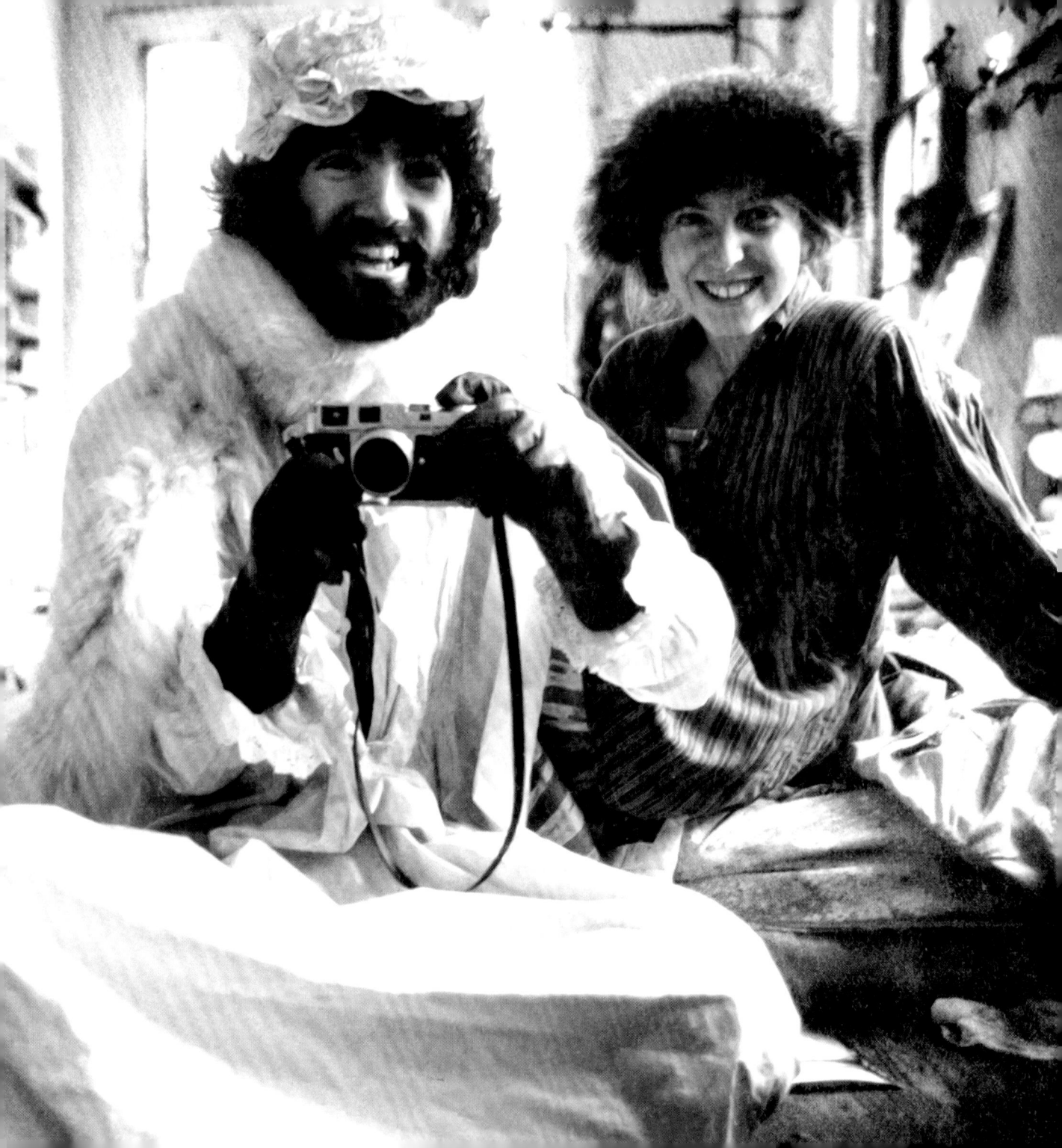

My classmate Francesca Woodman was the real deal. She lived her art. She looked like her art. She had the vocabulary of art. And the images she showed in class each week blew me away.

Francesca's short but brilliant career has had a dark cloud over it due to her death by suicide in her early twenties. But my friendship with her in college doesn't reflect that public perception—we were silly together. Francesca had this really high-pitched voice and a funny, mischievous laugh. She would send me little notes on scraps of fur to come to tea at her loft or mail me prints with cryptic messages.

THAT'S HOW I REMEMBER FRANCESCA.

Francesca wasn't just a tortured soul—in fact, I didn't know that person. That's partly because it's not the way that I see the world nor what I find in people. But truly, it was also because there was this other lighter side of her, too.

My first year of college, I had the chance to photograph Joni Mitchell in concert and got a single frame that was a stunner. I sold dozens of 8 x 10s of that image, which I signed and carefully dry mounted on boards, for ten or twenty dollars. That was my spending money as a freshman. For years after college, I would run into this picture in surprising places.

Once, I was looking for a place to stay on Martha's Vineyard. The owners of one rental property showed me the bedroom; there was my Joni Mitchell print smiling back at me. It was like running into an old friend.

Then, a couple of years ago, I was sitting alone at a New York sandwich shop, and a stranger sitting nearby asked me, "What's your name?" He thought I looked familiar. "George Lange," I replied. The guy then said, "That is so weird. I used to know a George Lange who was a photographer. I gave him a ride from Ithaca to Vassar, and he paid me with a Joni Mitchell print. I still have the photograph hanging in my house."

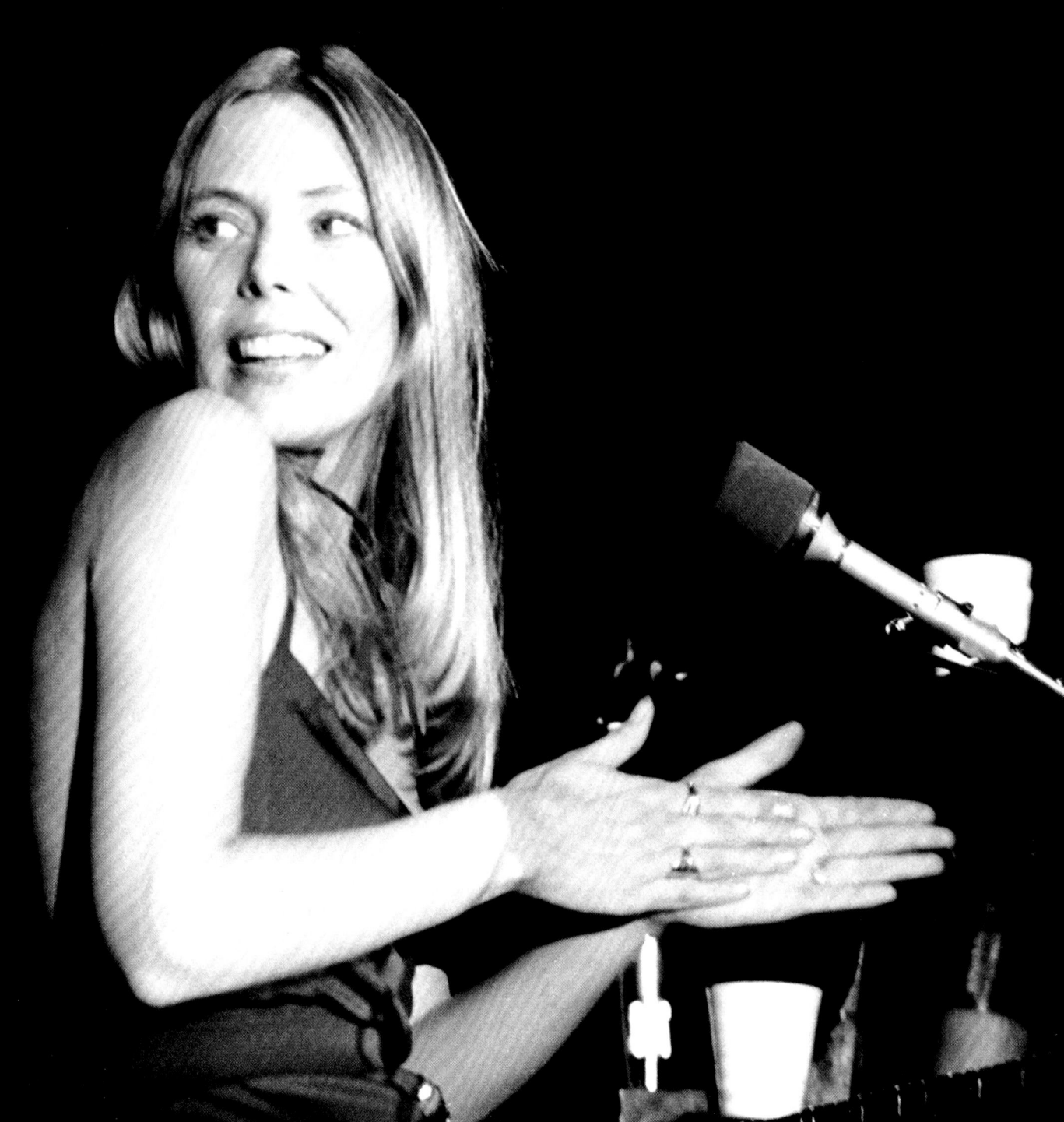

After graduation, I moved in to a seven-dollar-a-night room at the Y on Twenty-Third Street in New York City and got to work. I had an idea of where I wanted to be but no clue how to get there. I found a small door into the big room with one of my idols, Annie Leibovitz, and worked my way up to being her main assistant.

I traveled in a very different orbit when I was with her—literally. After one shoot, we took the supersonic Concorde from Paris to New York. I was thrilled because they advertised "unlimited caviar." I found out after multiple orders that it was, in fact, limited.

WHEN I THINK ABOUT WHAT I LEARNED FROM ANNIE,

I can sum it up with one word: rhythm. At the level that Annie was working, everyone communicates with a certain rhythm. It is almost like a shared language that has its own pace and tempo. The art directors, the top picture editors, and the subjects were all pushing themselves to be a part of creating something new and different. Being next to Annie for a year, I saw her navigate this dance close up.

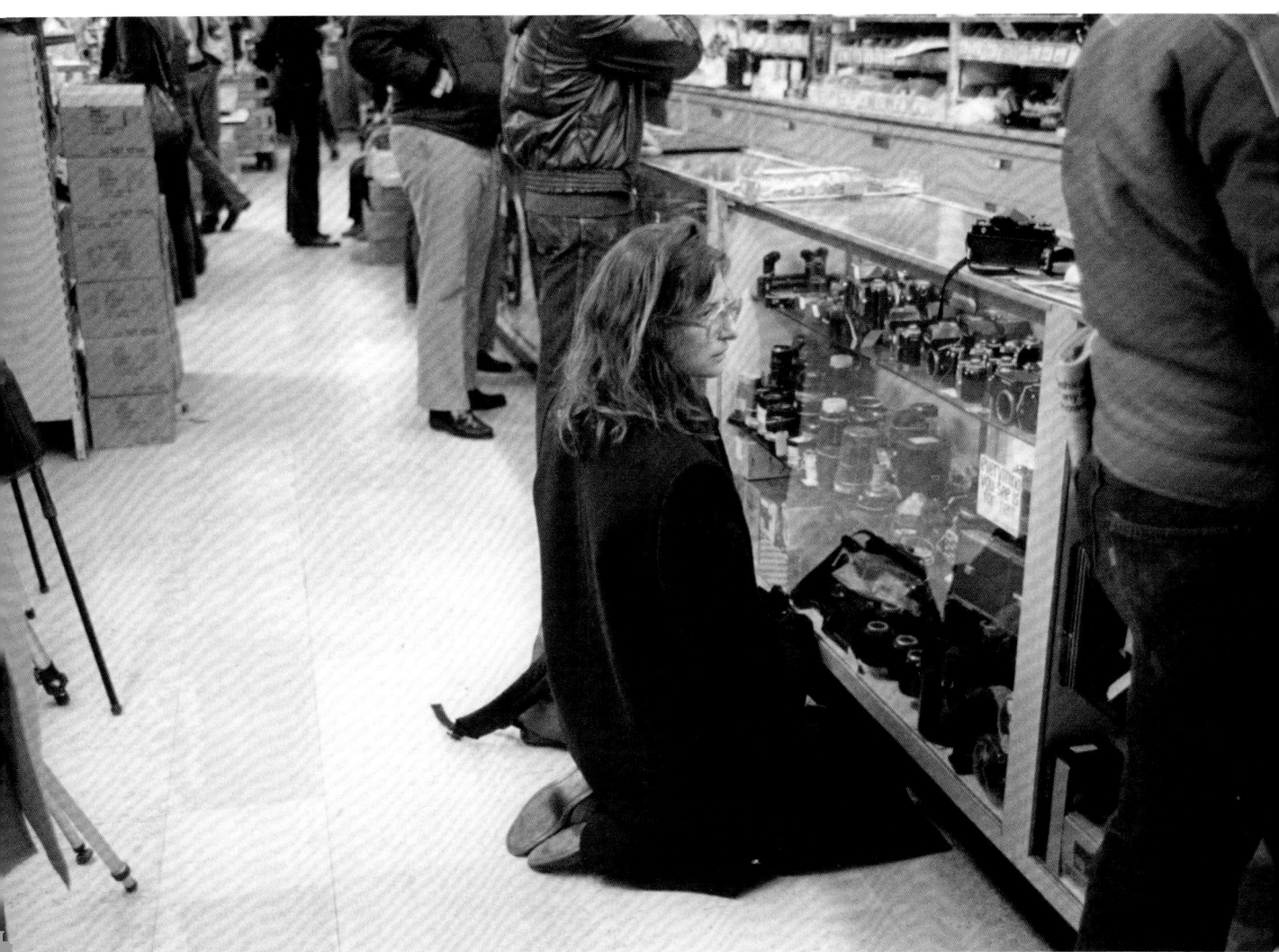

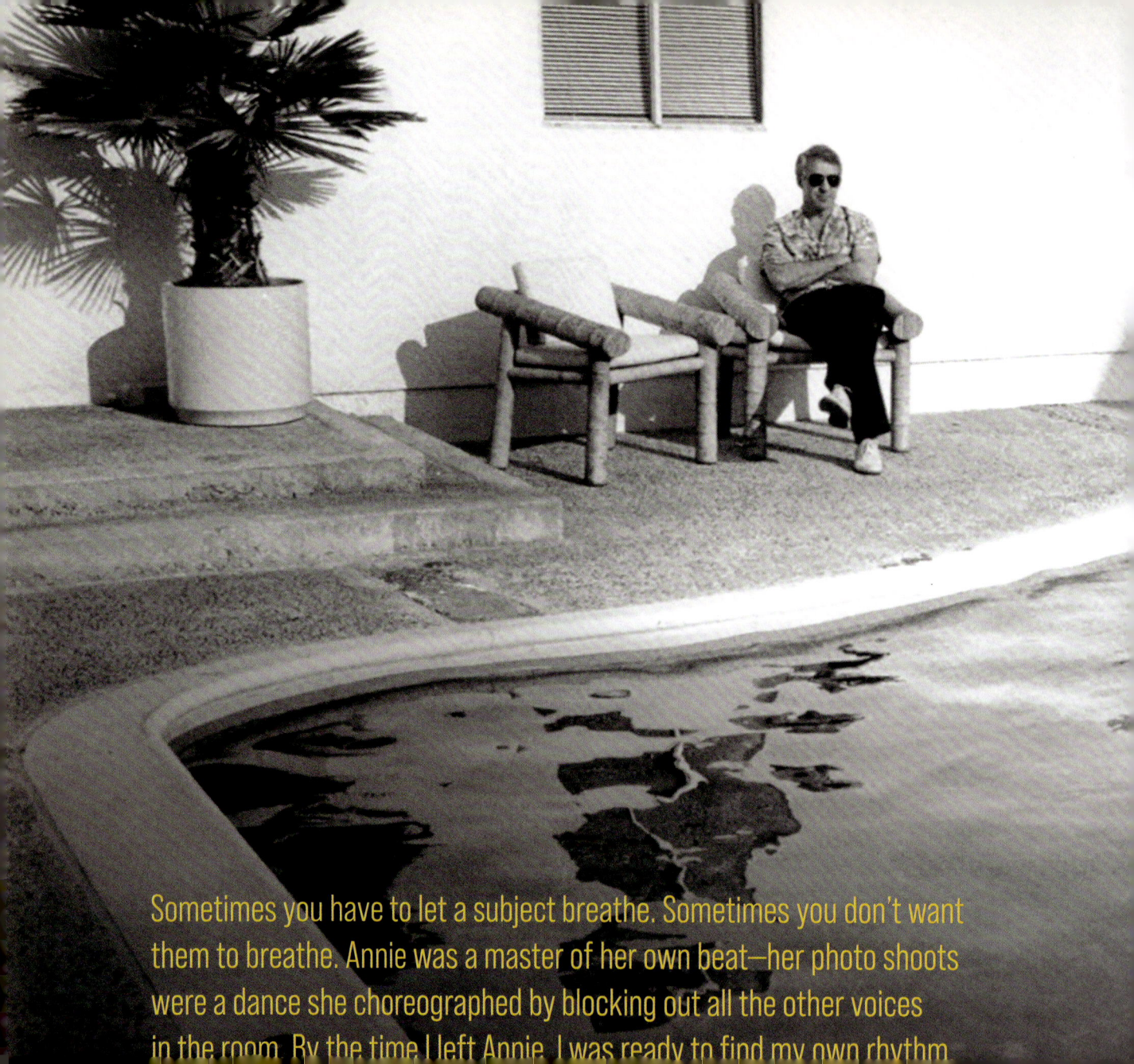

Sometimes you have to let a subject breathe. Sometimes you don't want them to breathe. Annie was a master of her own beat—her photo shoots were a dance she choreographed by blocking out all the other voices in the room. By the time I left Annie, I was ready to find my own rhythm

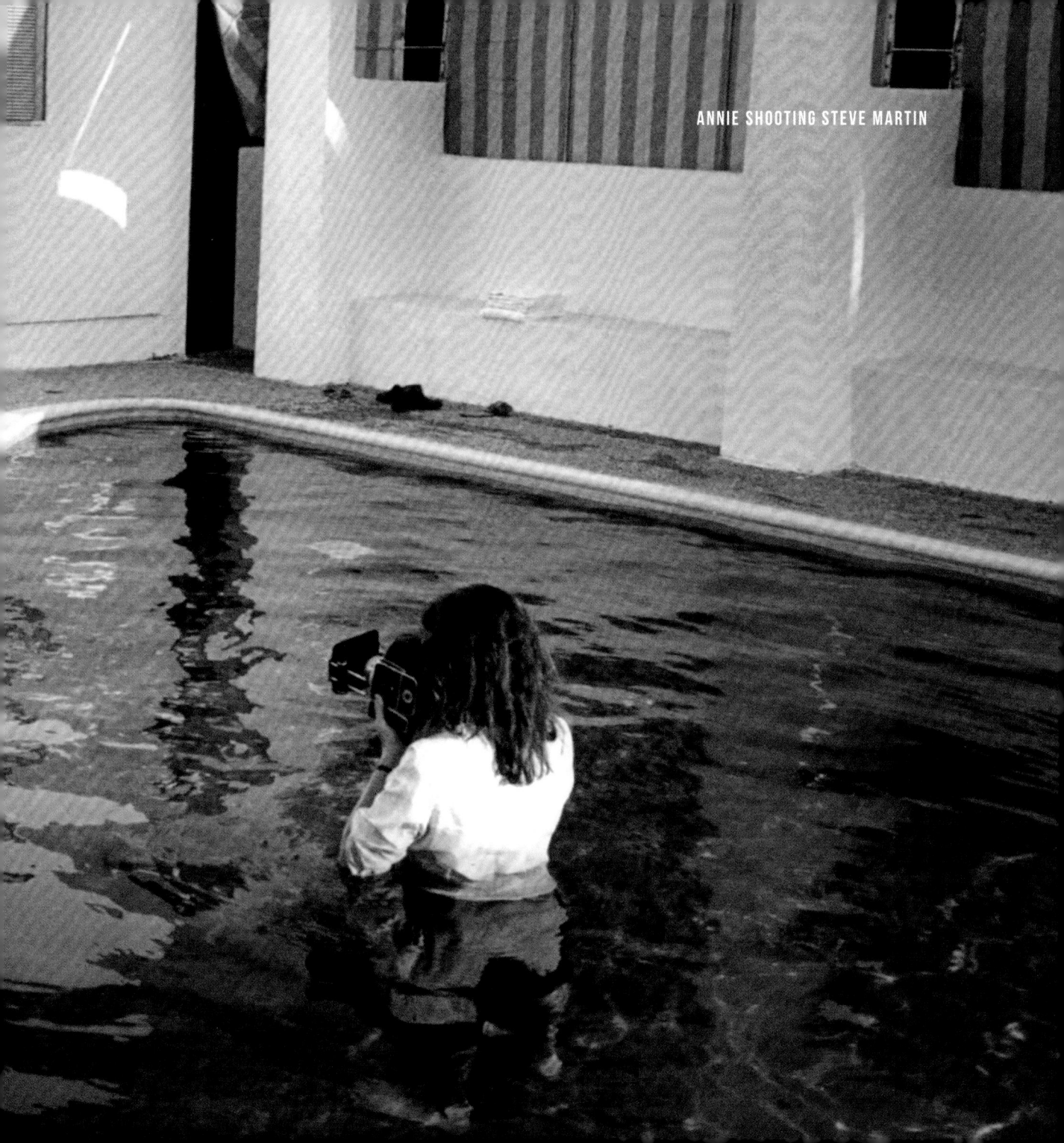

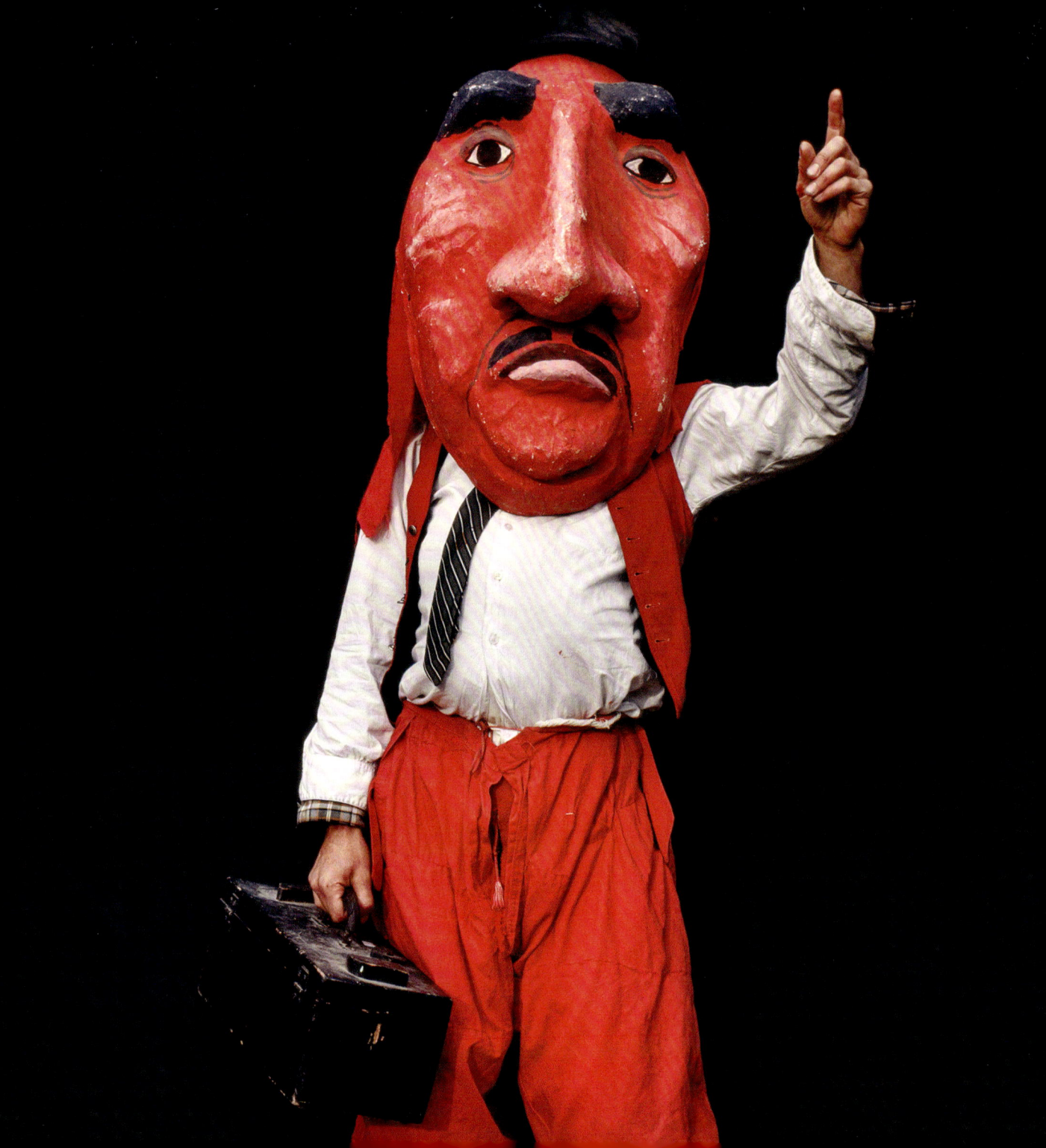

I had the opportunity to spend time with Bread and Puppet Theater, the incredible vision and creation of German anarchist, activist, and puppeteer Peter Schumann. I was able to bring my love of their work to the attention of *GEO* magazine, one of the top photo-driven magazines in the world. *GEO*'s picture editor at the time, Elisabeth Biondi, took a chance on this very young, very enthusiastic photographer. I have no idea how she thought this was a good plan. (I asked her recently and she still couldn't answer that question!)

The theater was political and strange and brilliant. But one thing it was not was photo friendly. The puppeteers allowed their performances to be documented, but they never wanted to interact or pose. I drove to northern Vermont, where Bread and Puppet was based, with no money and the knowledge that I had rarely shot in color before.

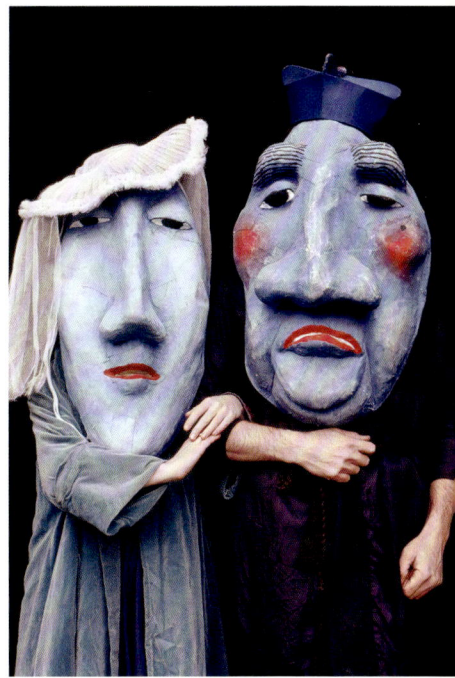

For weeks, I went back and forth between New York and Vermont. Gaining the company's trust was the real key. Knowing how hard to push and when to blend in to the scenery was something this photographer still needed to learn. Even though I was getting good shots, I hadn't captured the cover image that *GEO* wanted.

After working on the story for over three months, I was totally out of money. If the story were killed, I would have to leave New York.

The northern Vermont winter was setting in. The days were getting shorter, darker, and colder. I tried to get my posed shots for several days with no luck. On my last day, I put up a piece of black fabric on the outside wall of the barn and begged them, "Please! Would you just stand in front of it for me?"

The sun was setting when the puppeteers finally agreed to put on their giant masks and stand in front of my makeshift backdrop for a couple of moments. I had one camera, one lens, and one sliver of fading light to get the shots. I thanked them, said goodbye, and packed up.

Back in New York, I presented the new photos to the top editors at *GEO*. The mood in the room was tense—especially for me, knowing my whole future was riding on their decision. When I showed the work . . . applause broke out. My story was accepted.

IT RAN FOR FOURTEEN PAGES, AND A PUPPET IN A VEIL AND A PINK DRESS, AGAINST THAT BLACK FABRIC, WAS THE COVER OF THE MARCH 1983 ISSUE OF THE MAGAZINE.

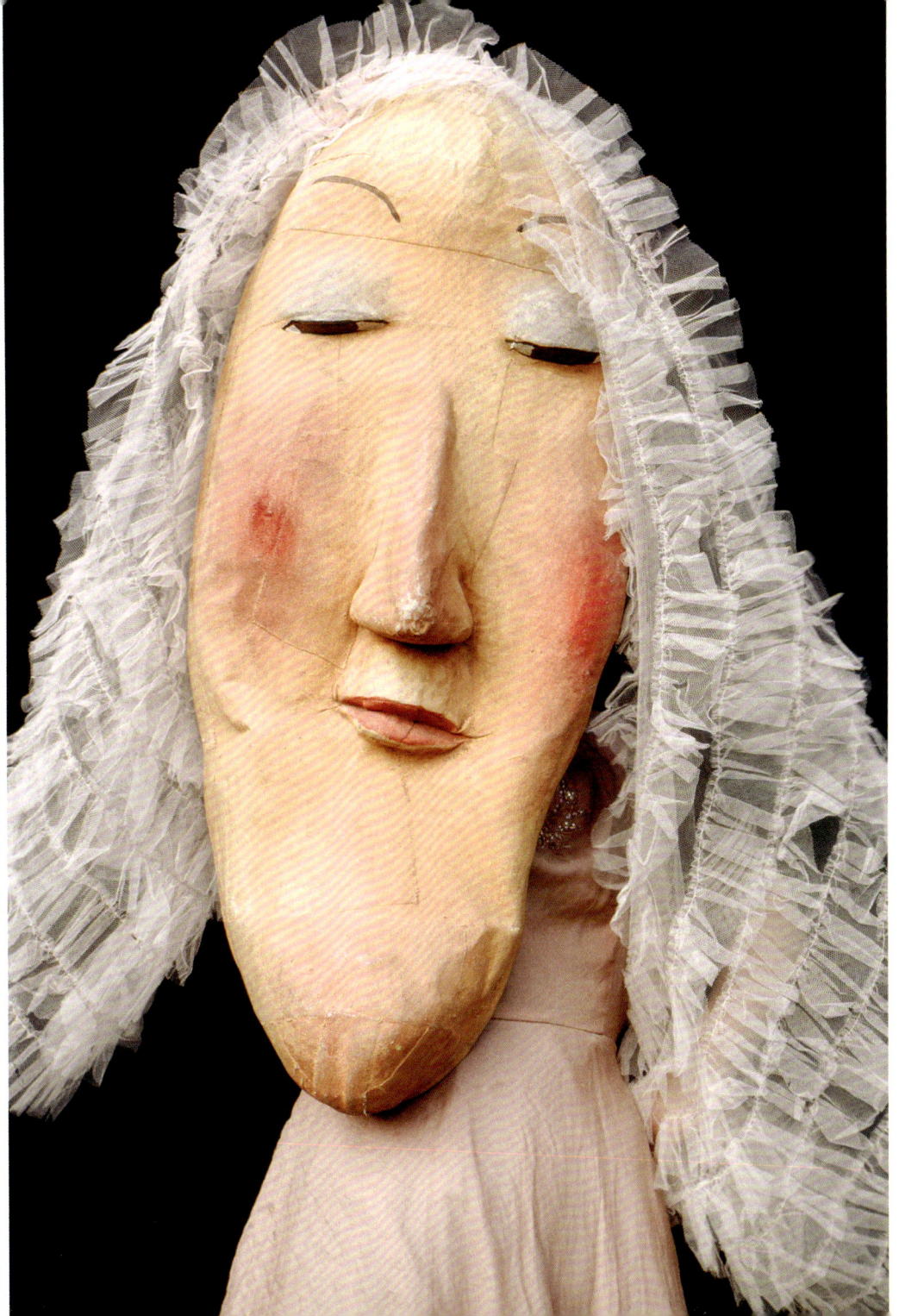

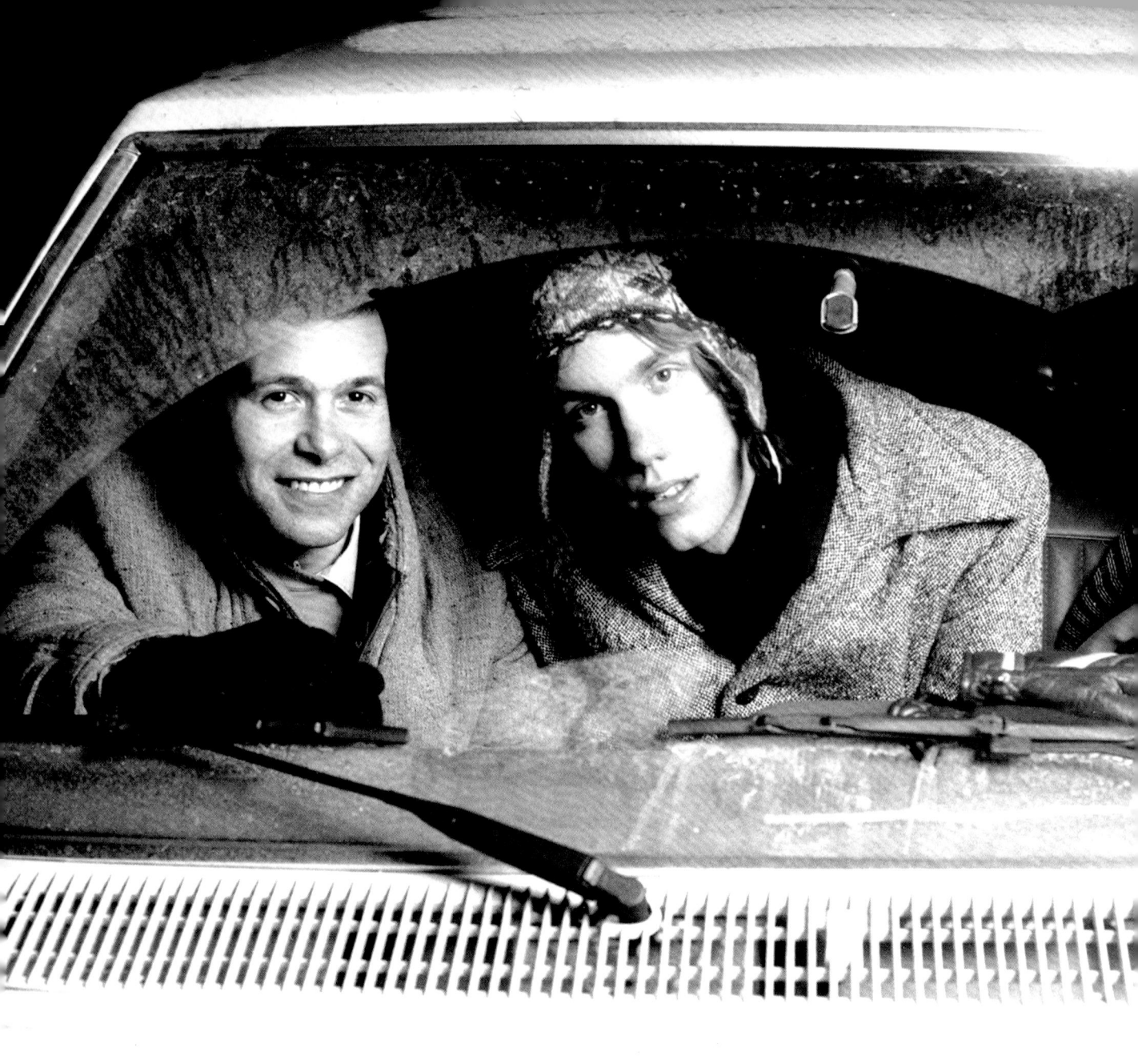

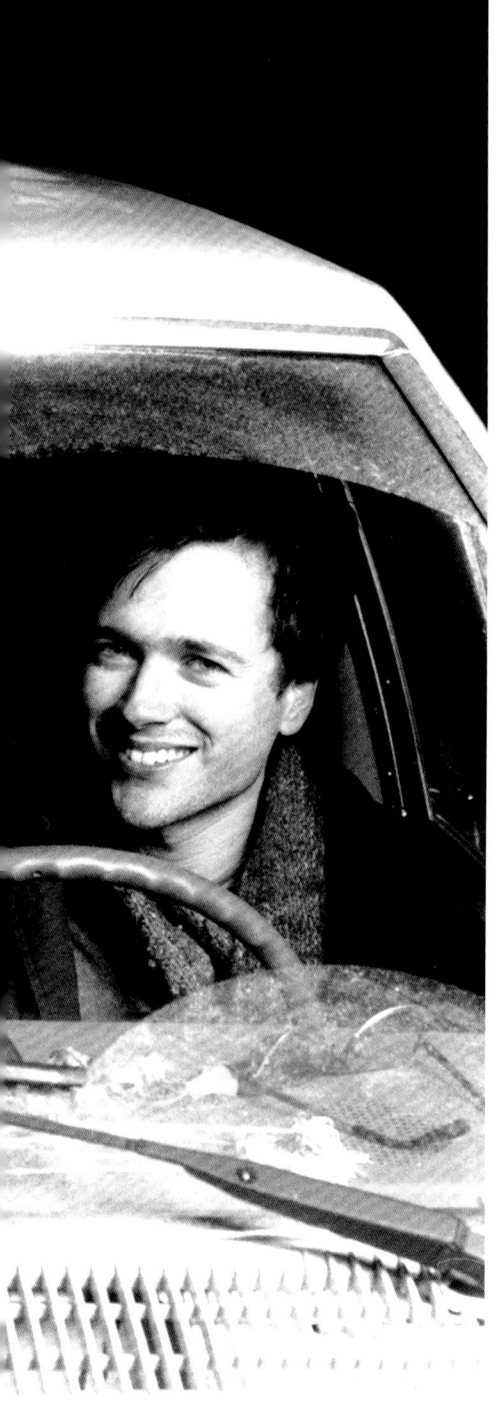

My first assignment for *Rolling Stone* was to shoot the punk band Violent Femmes. I think I was getting seventy-five dollars for the whole assignment, but it was a huge deal for me. I went to meet them in Brooklyn with one strobe light, my 35 mm camera, and no assistant. When I started setting up, my strobe would not fire. Soon it was dark and I was a wreck. Instead of giving up, we planned a trip for me to visit them in Milwaukee a week later.

I flew to Chicago and found a place that would rent me a car with cash—I didn't have a credit card—and drove to Wisconsin. Victor, the drummer, put me up. We took pictures on and off for three days. One freezing night we did a photo shoot up on an abandoned highway with the band bundled up inside their car, trying to stay warm.

I set up a light outside and jumped on the front of their car in the hope of getting something good. The strobe was blowing in the cold, and I couldn't see inside the car, so this picture only existed in my mind until I saw the developed film a week later. I was trying to play rock photographer, but I was really only at the very beginning of my career.

Being a photographer is like learning to drive a stick shift when you are stopped in the middle of a hill. You need to find that sweet spot of giving the car a little gas and letting out the clutch, rocking it carefully and trying not to roll backward. The goal is to just keep it moving forward while not stalling out.

Some shoots require a lot of direction and help. Others need you to sit back and take it all in and not mess it up. The more cerebral the subject, the more direction you'll need to give. The more physical subjects—dancers, certain comedians, most young kids, athletes—you can follow their lead. The important part for me is creating a space to learn from my subject. This is a collaboration. If it is only about "my vision," it is not as interesting.

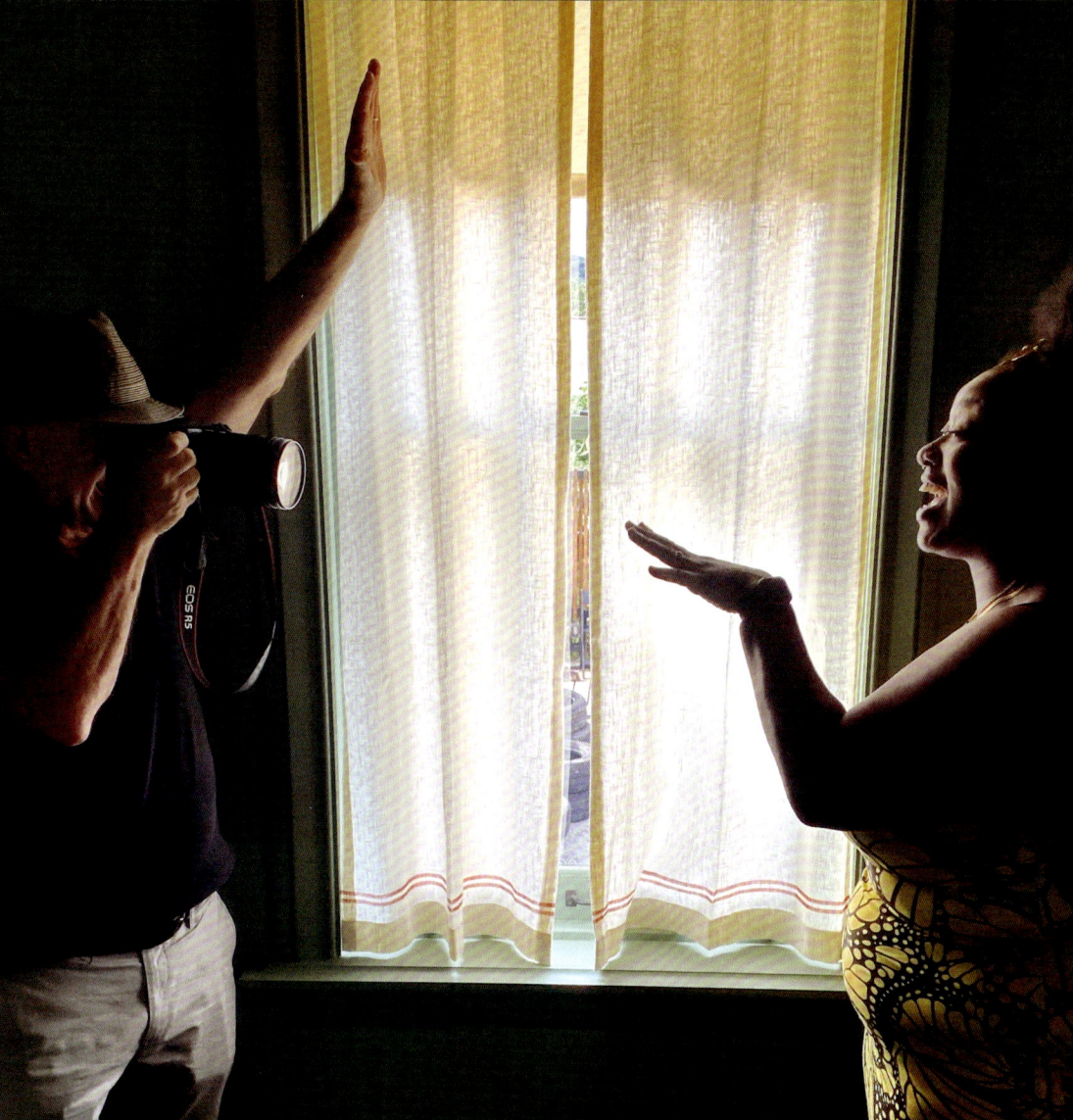

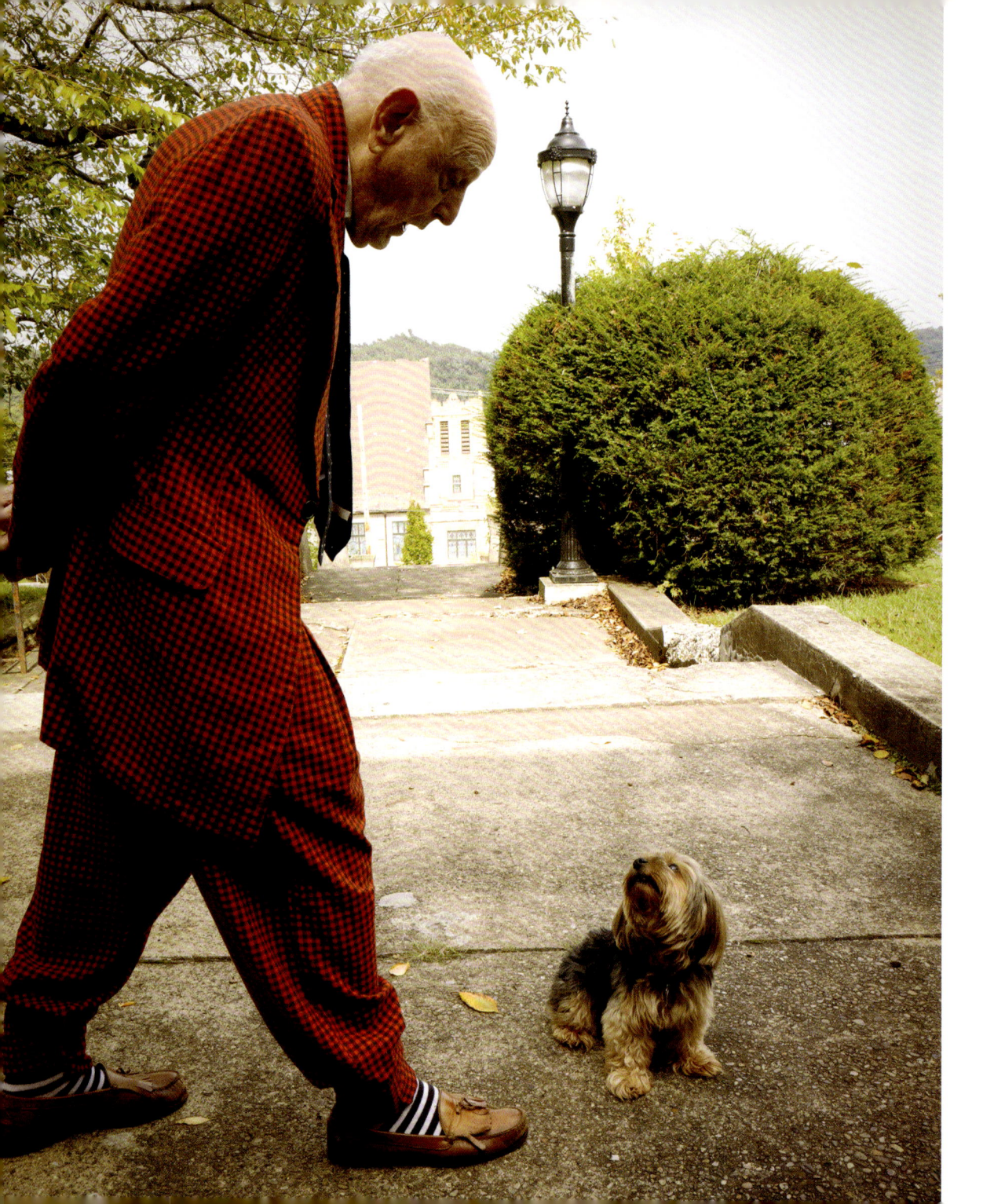

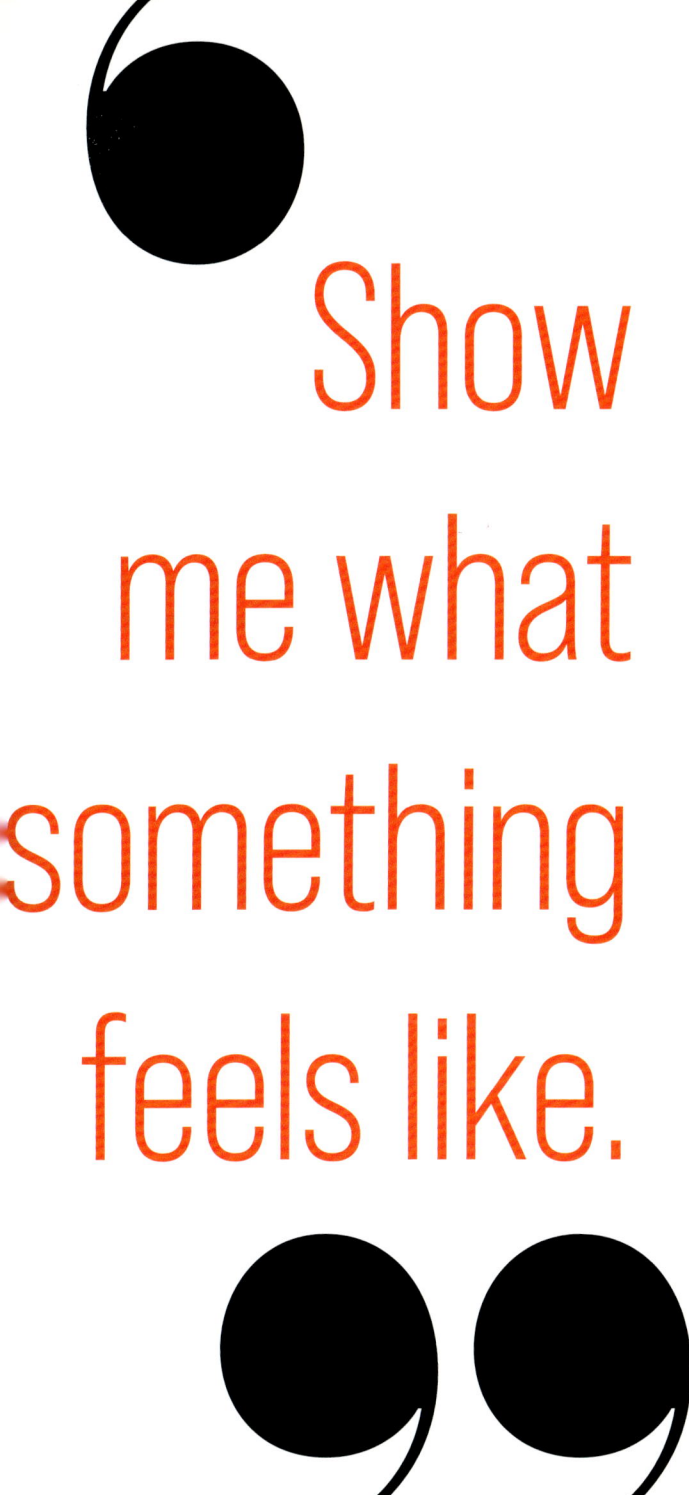

Show me what something feels like.

It is a funny dance we do with our heroes. I consider fellow Pittsburgher Duane Michals to be the greatest living photographer. My relationship with him goes back forty-five years, but only in the past few years have I gotten over my intimidation enough to become his friend.

When I was at RISD, I went to hear Duane speak at MIT. The minute I sat down, I pulled out my little cassette recorder. He spoke fast, and the recorder was far away from the stage, but it was enough to capture the lecture.

I spent the next week transcribing the talk for myself on a legal pad. It became my creative bible, a way to have Duane whisper his wisdom in my ear. Two of the greatest lessons I've learned from him are "Don't show me what I already know" and "Show me what something feels like."

I called Duane when I came to New York and got to assist him on a one-day shoot for *Vogue*. I carried his lights in a beach bag and grabbed his tripod. Mostly I just pinched myself all day, full of disbelief that I got to watch him work. Outside of that day, I would occasionally run into Duane on the street in New York City. He would say, "George, call me. I'm in the phone book." But I couldn't do it—he was such a big deal to me.

When I finally did, we became great friends. I guess it was time for Duane to join the ongoing conversation I'd been having in my mind with him all of those years.

My favorite rule that ninety-one-year-old Duane lives by is:

"IF YOU HAVE AN IDEA ON MONDAY, HAVE IT DONE BY FRIDAY."

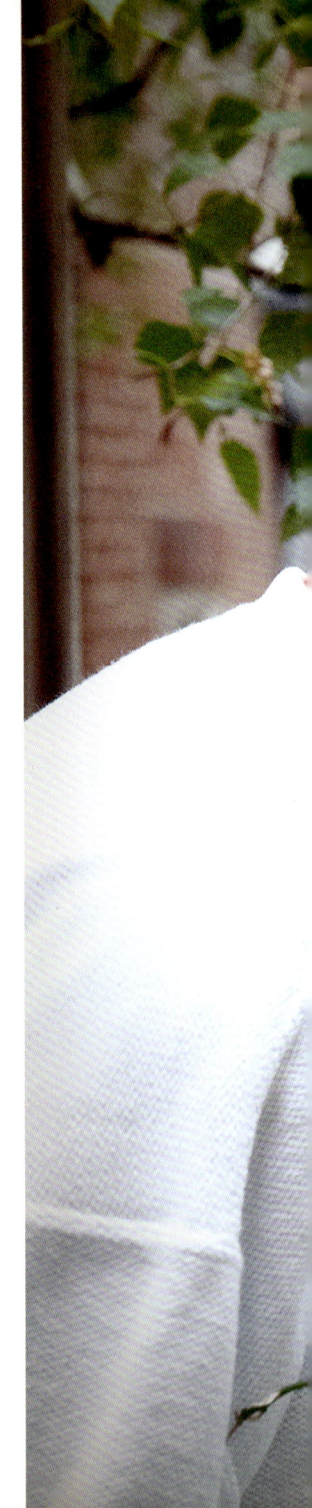

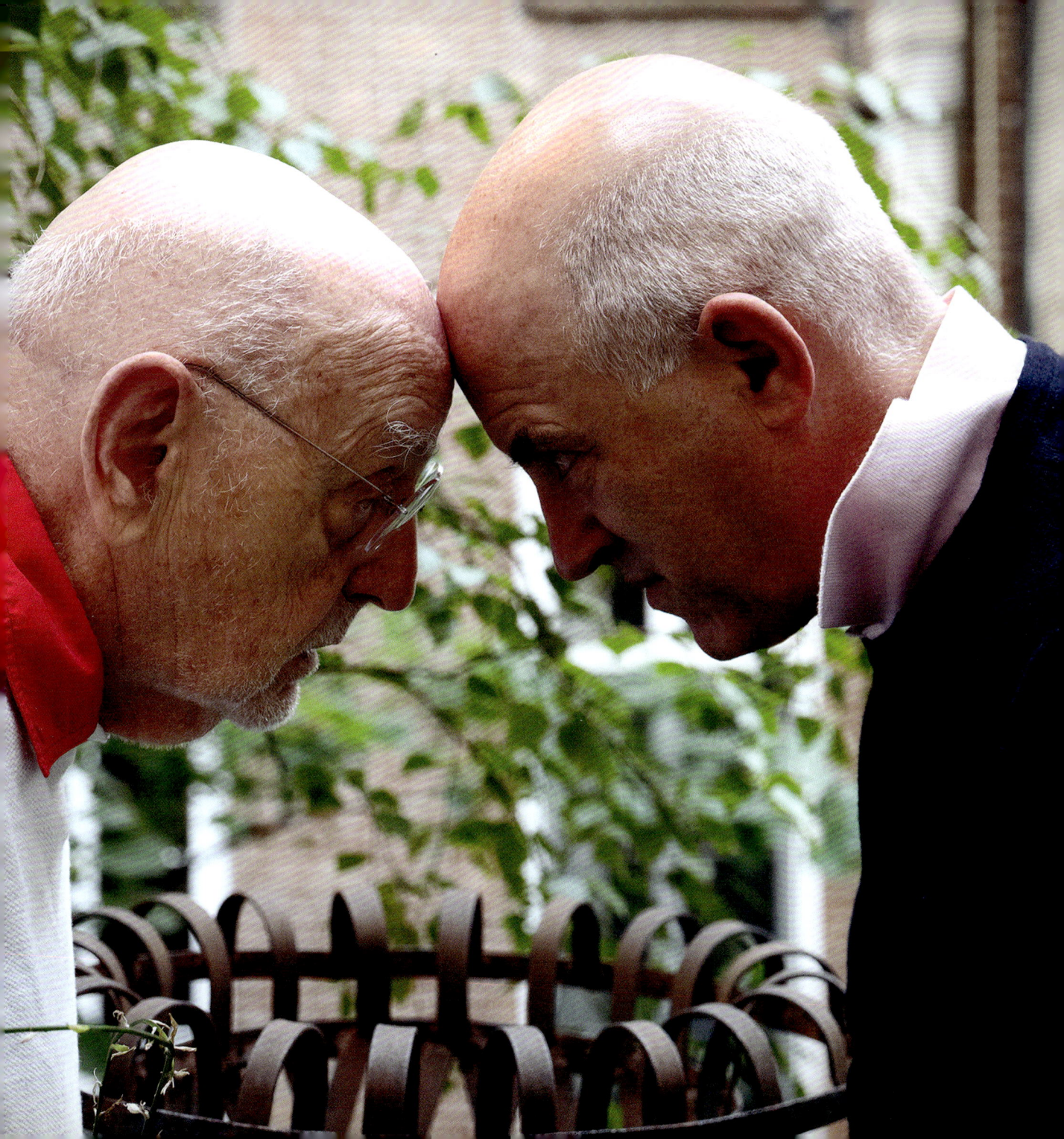

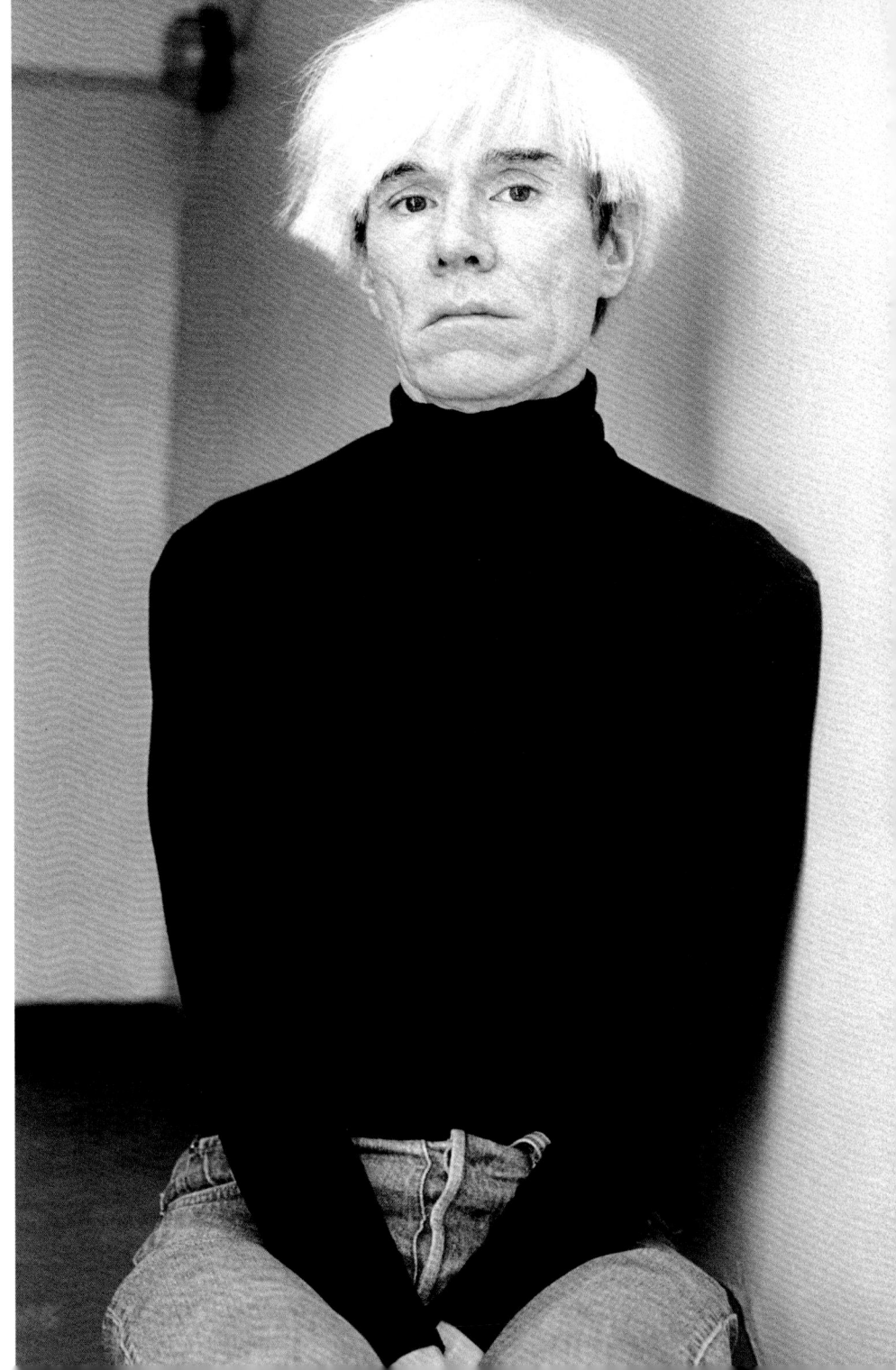

Early in my career, I got an amazing assignment for *Decoration Internationale*, a French interiors magazine. It was a black-and-white shoot of twenty high-society New York subjects, from Paloma Picasso to Alexander Liberman to Andy Warhol.

For Andy, I showed up at the Factory on Broadway. Aluminum foil covered the walls. He didn't talk to me, even though we were both natives of Pittsburgh. We went to a nondescript room to shoot. It didn't occur to me that he was wearing a wig. Andy went into the bathroom, left the door open, and leaned up on the sink to carefully groom his nose hairs. Then he was ready.

I took some shots of him sitting on a table and some by a window in the stairwell. While I was certainly curious about him, I suddenly was completely at a loss for words—which is not like me at all! I think Andy was good at intimidation, but I still got the photos I needed.

After my fifteen minutes with Andy Warhol were published, the entire shoot stayed tucked away in storage for many years. Recently, I unearthed the photos, and now he looks at me from my studio wall every day. I still don't know what to say to him.

Spike Lee's office is in Fort Greene, near the

same neighborhood of Brooklyn where he grew up.

When I arrived, a bunch of little kids were playing

outside and inspired me to include them in the

shoot. I thought they all could be Spike Lee one day.

Spike rarely laughs for photos, so I love how happy

he is in the middle of all these kids.

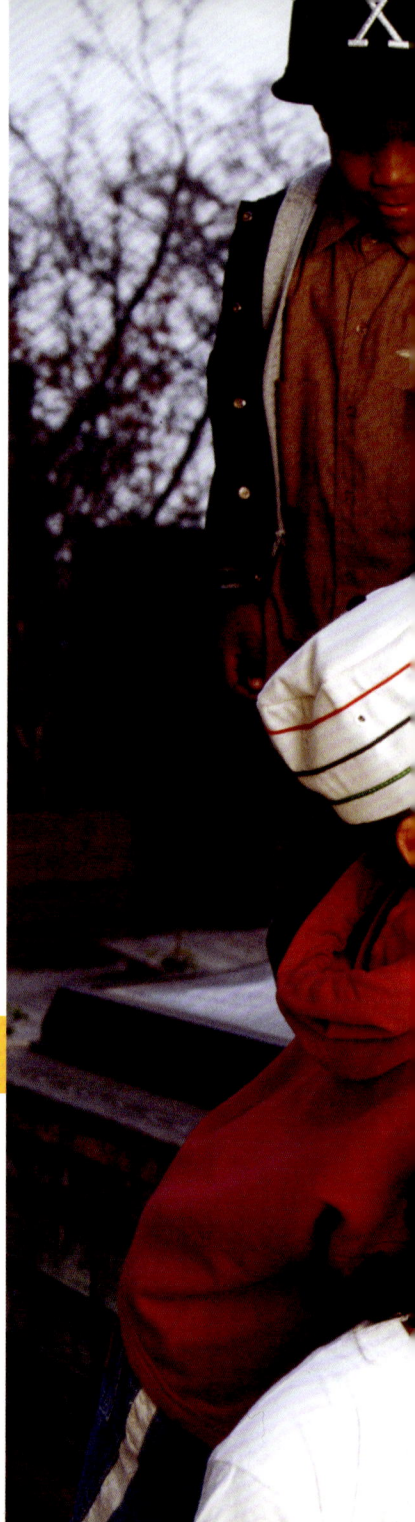

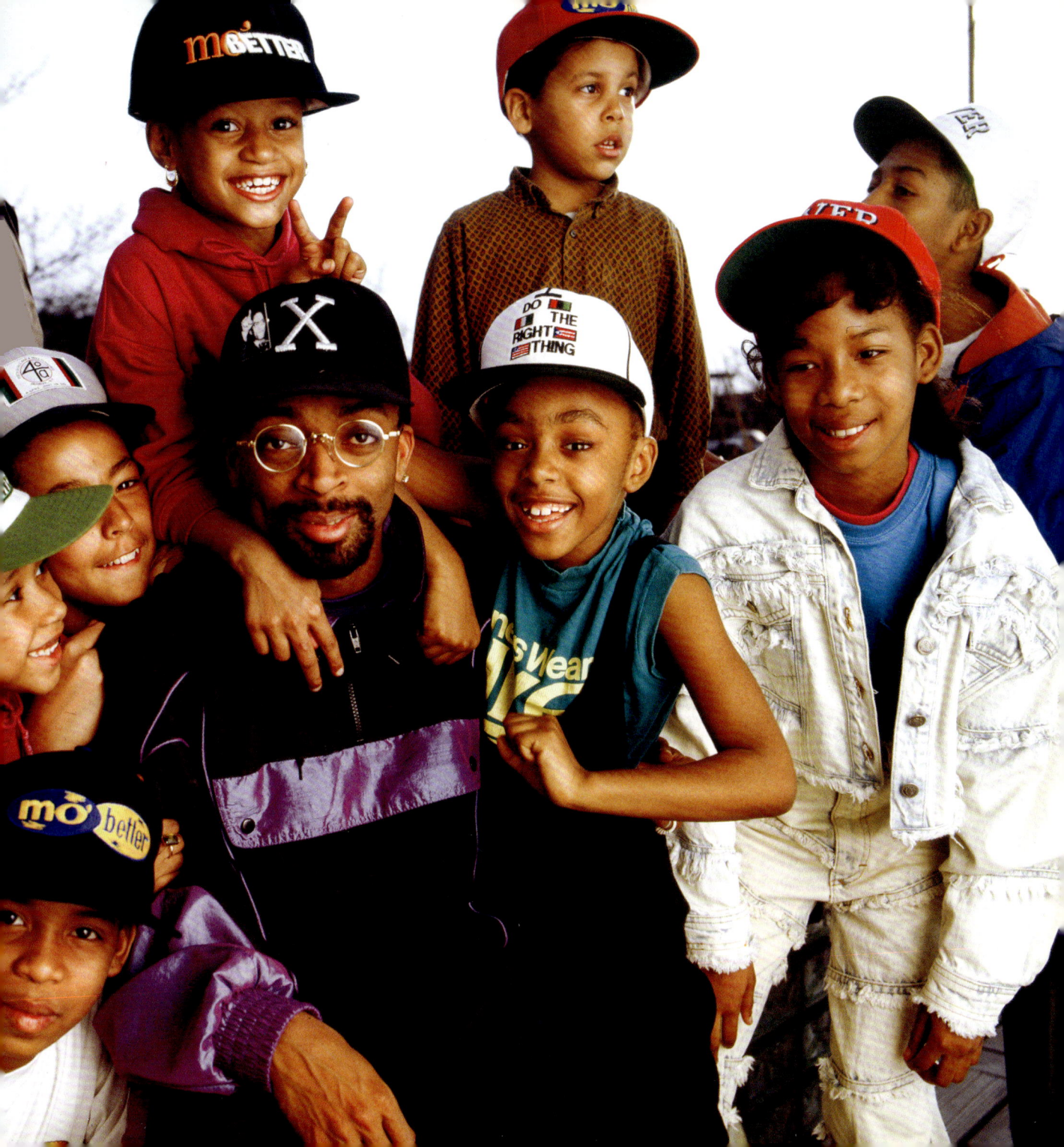

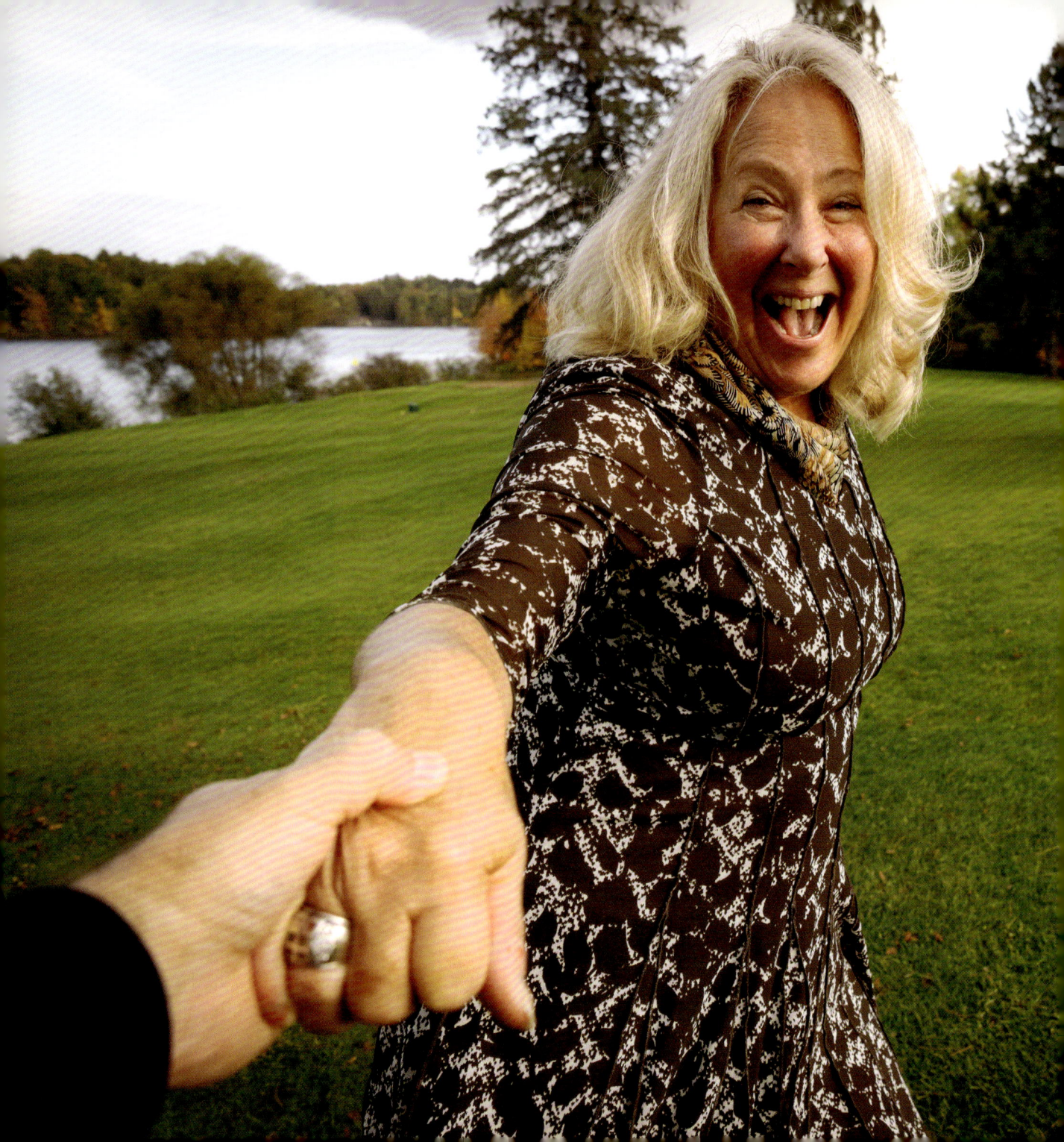

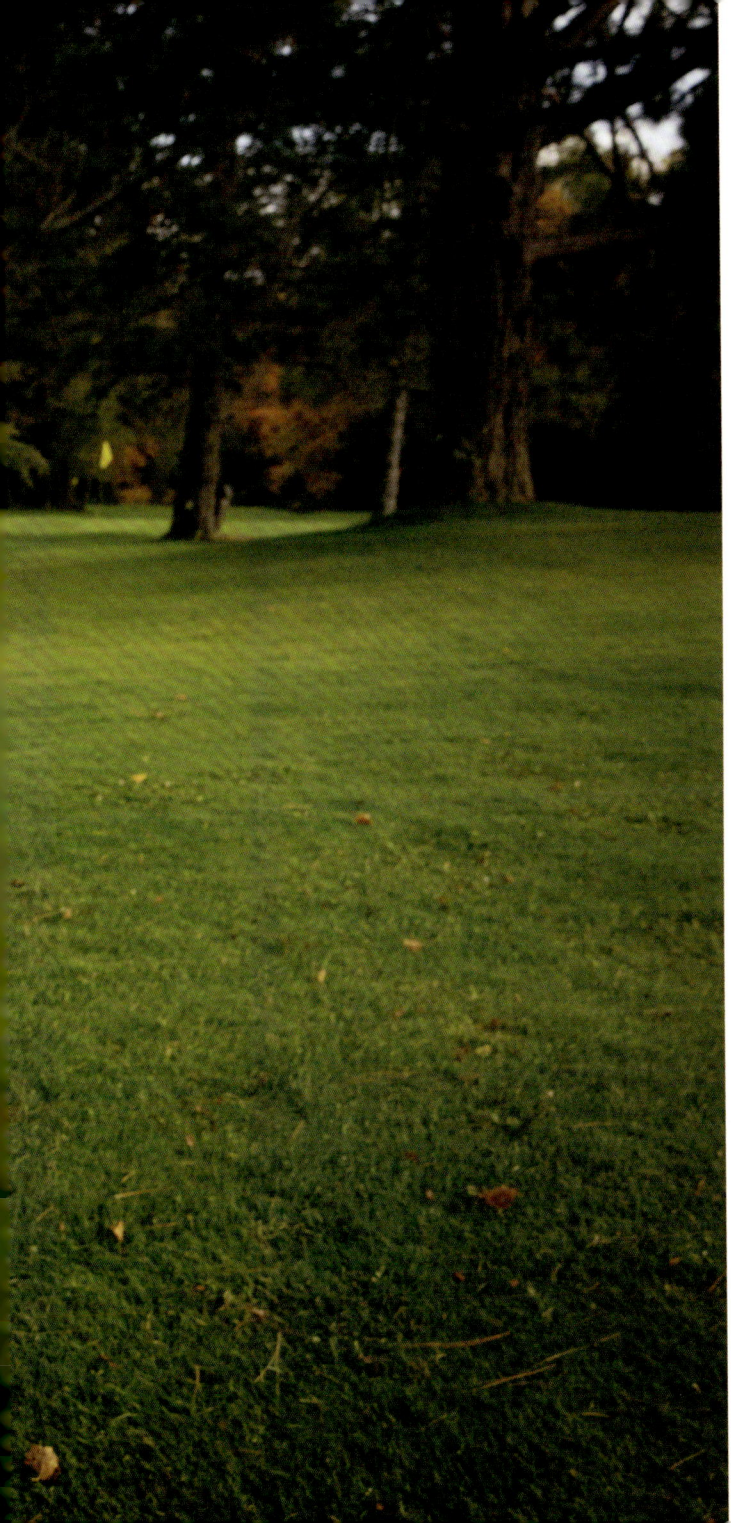

Sometimes my subjects struggle when we start taking pictures. It is not normal to look into a camera and pose for a portrait. It is in those moments that I need to help them connect with me.

Often, I hold my camera with one hand and hold the subject's hand with the other. Sometimes I just squeeze their hand. Sometimes we both lean back and spin around. It always allows us to connect. Everything feels alive, and nothing is more beautiful than that.

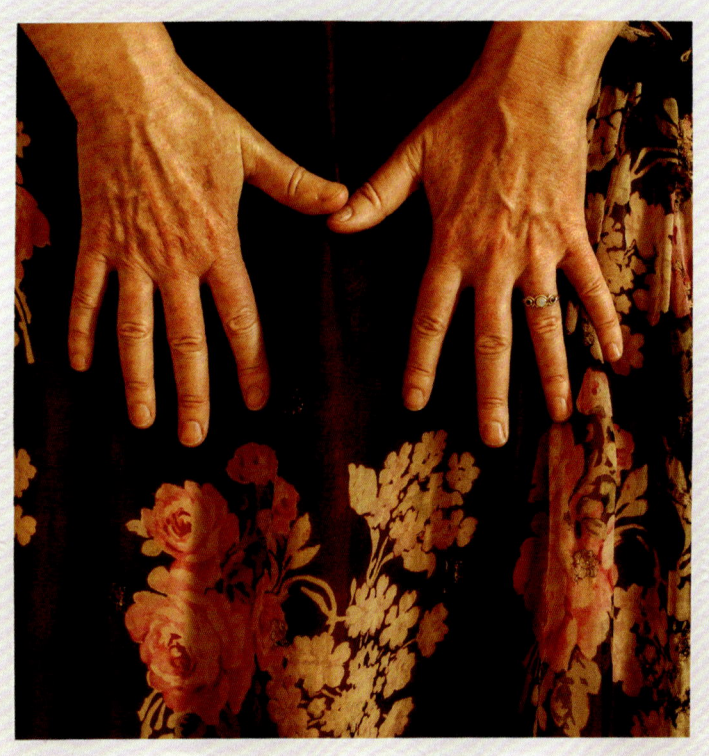

I photographed the writer Edna O'Brien in her hotel

room. I had taken a Polaroid of her hands resting on

the beautiful fabric of her dress. She asked if she could

take that picture to her lunch date.

An hour later, I was sitting on the floor, waiting for

her to return, when there was a tap on my shoulder.

A soft voice whispered inches from my ear, "I love the

photo you took of Edna's hands." I didn't recognize the

woman so close up, but as she moved away, I realized

it was Jackie O.

During a wild two-day marathon shoot in San Francisco for Twilio, the tech coding giant, I was given a small room, where we squeezed in two sets. There were signs everywhere sending people to be photographed by "Internationally renowned photographer George Lange" (that was a first!), and a constant queue outside of my space. We photographed 160 people in two days.

What could have been a stressful blur turned into a playground, where everyone reached out and held my hand. The music was loud, as it always has to be. The energy was infectious, so everyone could catch it. I wanted to make each person who stood before my lens feel for those moments that they were the only one who existed in the world.

I couldn't see much when I was taking the pictures, but I could feel everyone.

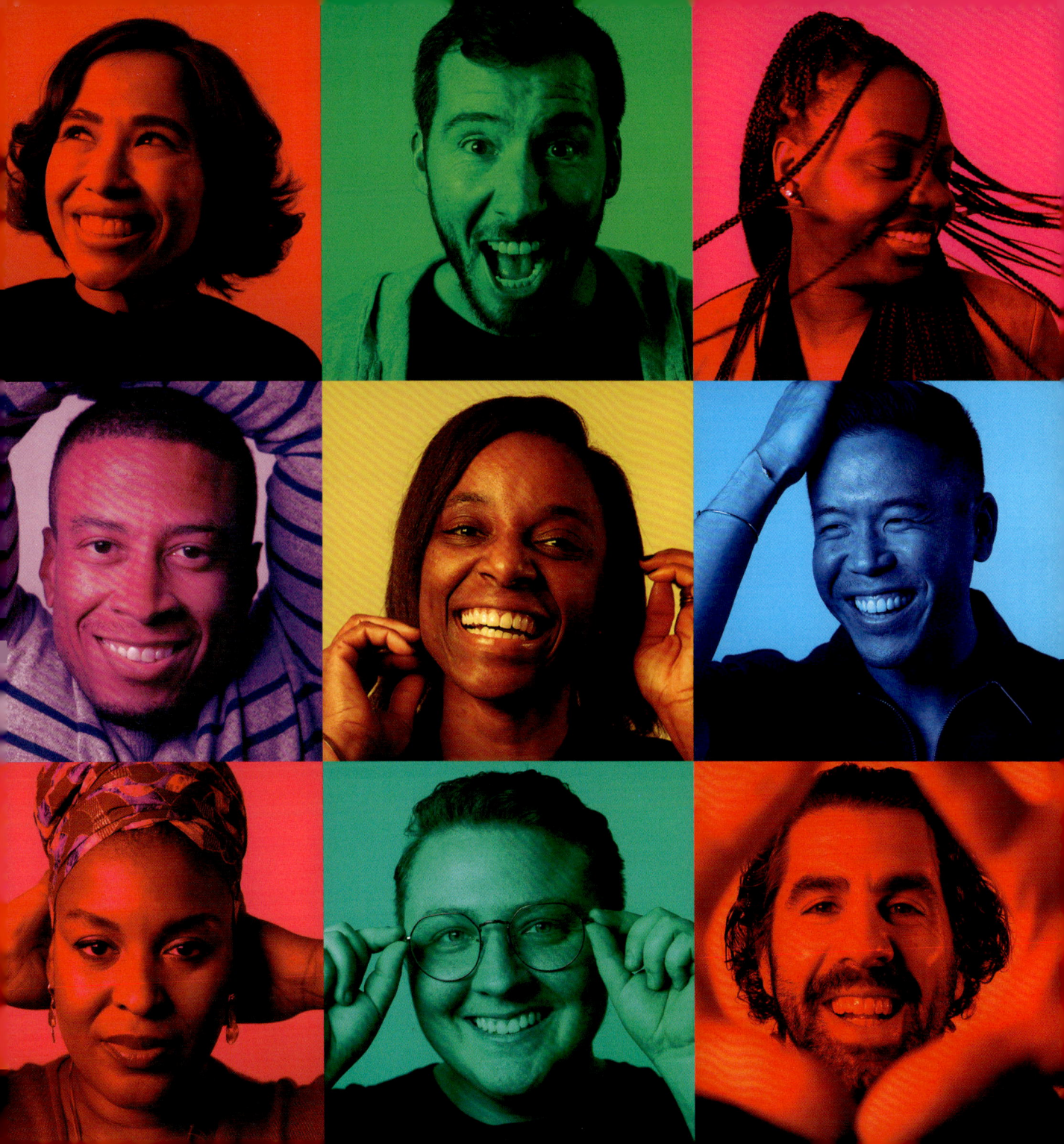

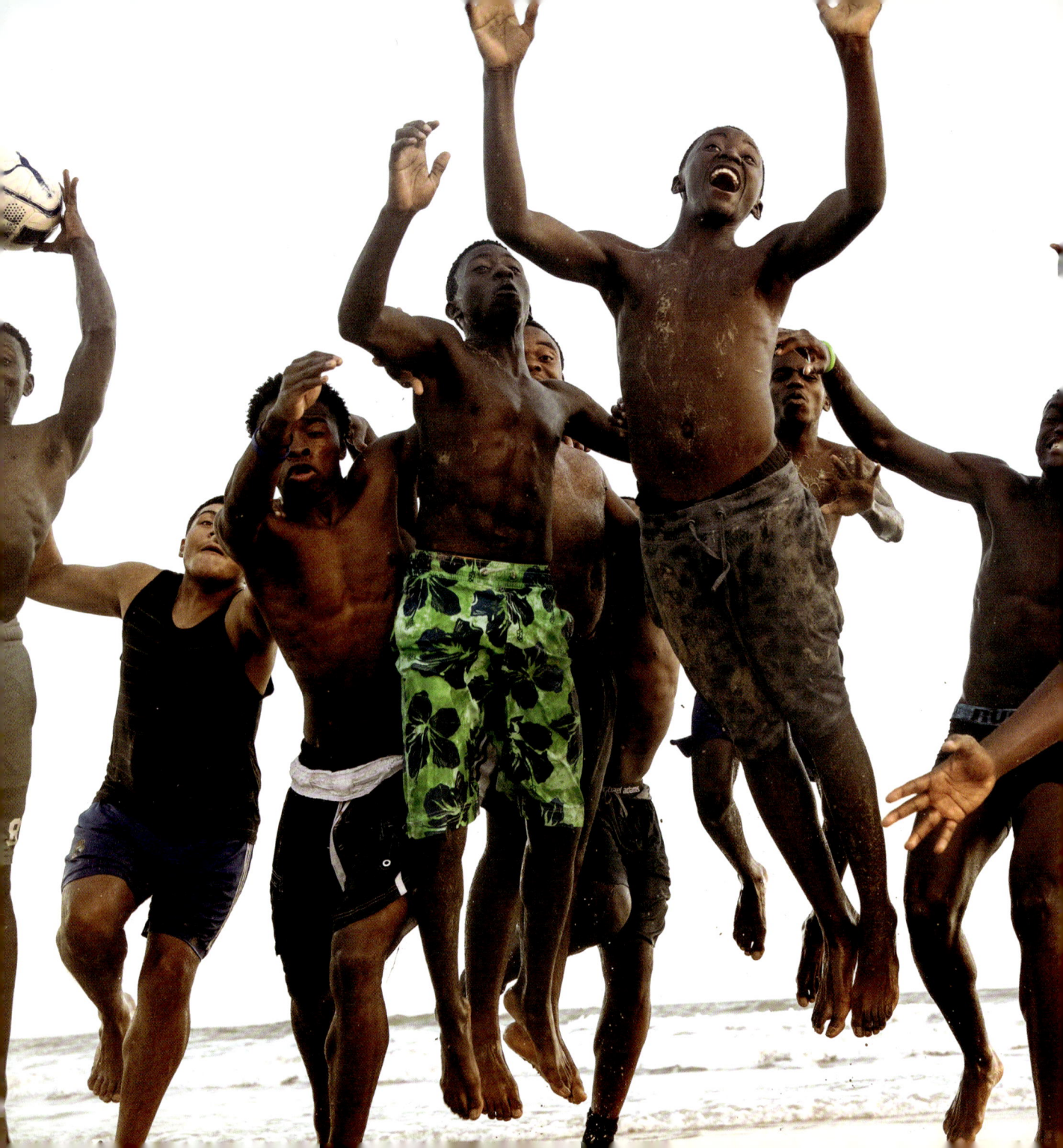

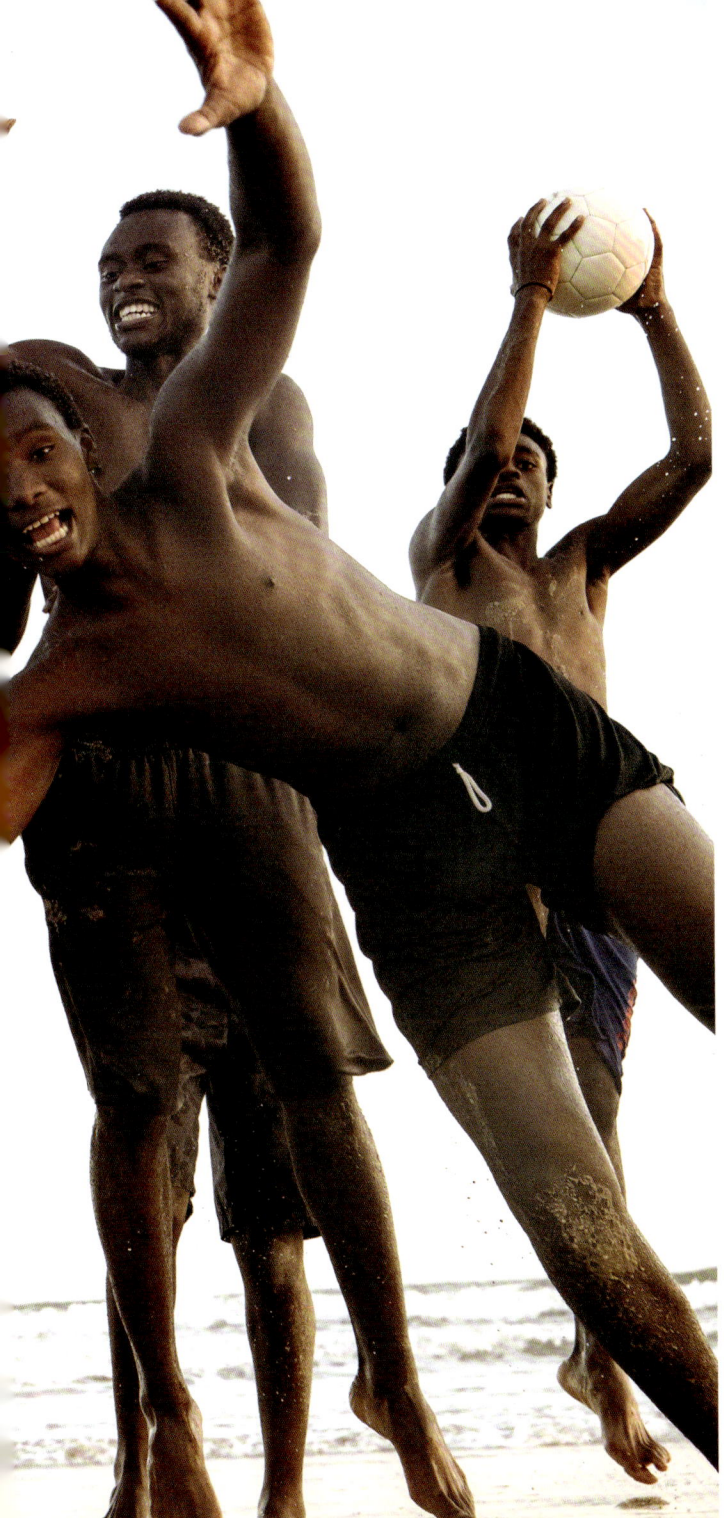

Sometimes taking photos is like capturing pure joy in my open hands. When a young group of refugees from Congo formed a soccer team in Houston, I wanted to photograph them on their very first visit to the beach, snapping shots as they kicked up the sand and flew over the waves.

Sharing the photos with them was even better. I printed the pictures and put them on their lockers as a surprise. When they came into the locker room and saw the photos, we all ended up in tears. It is my favorite exhibit of my photos ever.

Most of the time I know very little about my subjects before photographing them. I don't do research. I don't watch their movies or TV shows. I don't want to idolize them. Fear often handicaps us instead of motivating us.

I took this picture of John Lurie in New York before I really knew much about him except for his music. I have since seen his recent, wonderfully strange documentary series, *Painting with John*. His music is the soundtrack, which I love. His paintings are mysteries that I want to own. Lurie's days are so simple yet filled with everyday fun, like rolling a tire down a hill, crashing his drone, or wondering what it would be like to be an elephant. These days I get really inspired seeing his creations. Looking back at my picture of him, the whole shoot seems completely and perfectly naive.

The funny thing is, even after all the people I have photographed, I still get intimidated and kind of scared when I start a shoot.

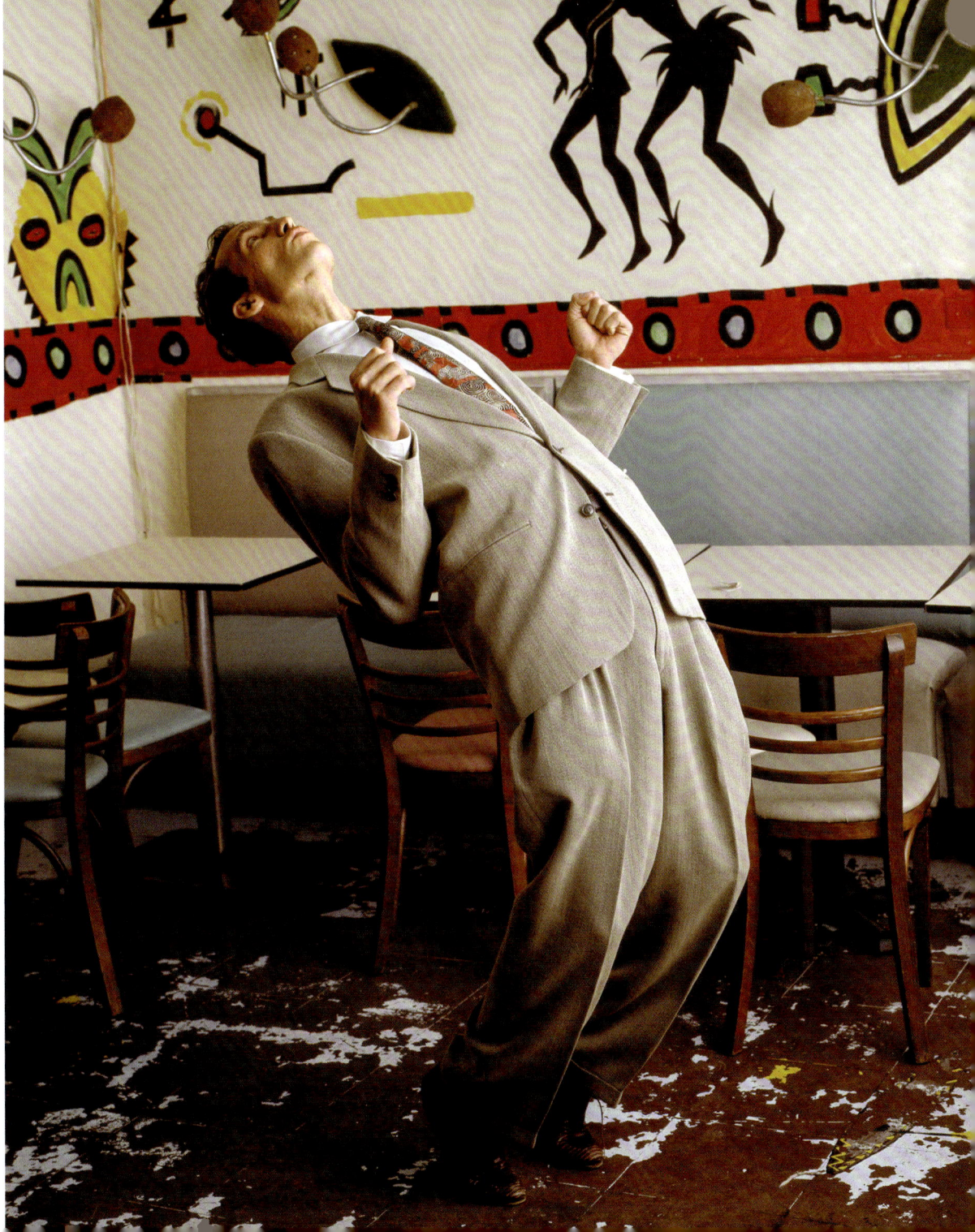

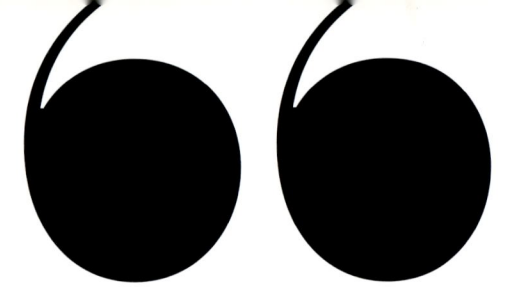

When I first saw Stephie in the doorway, I knew right away.

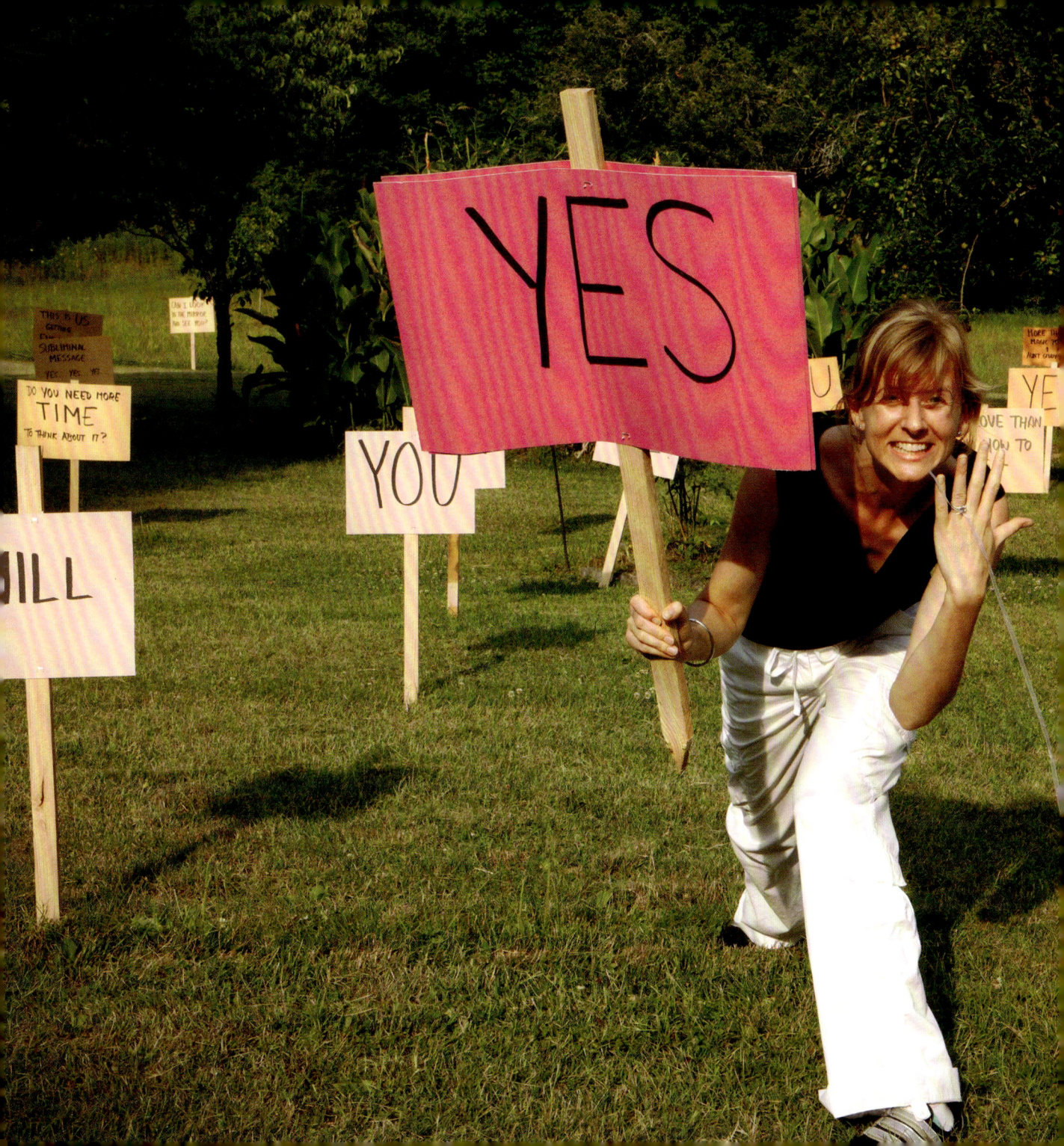

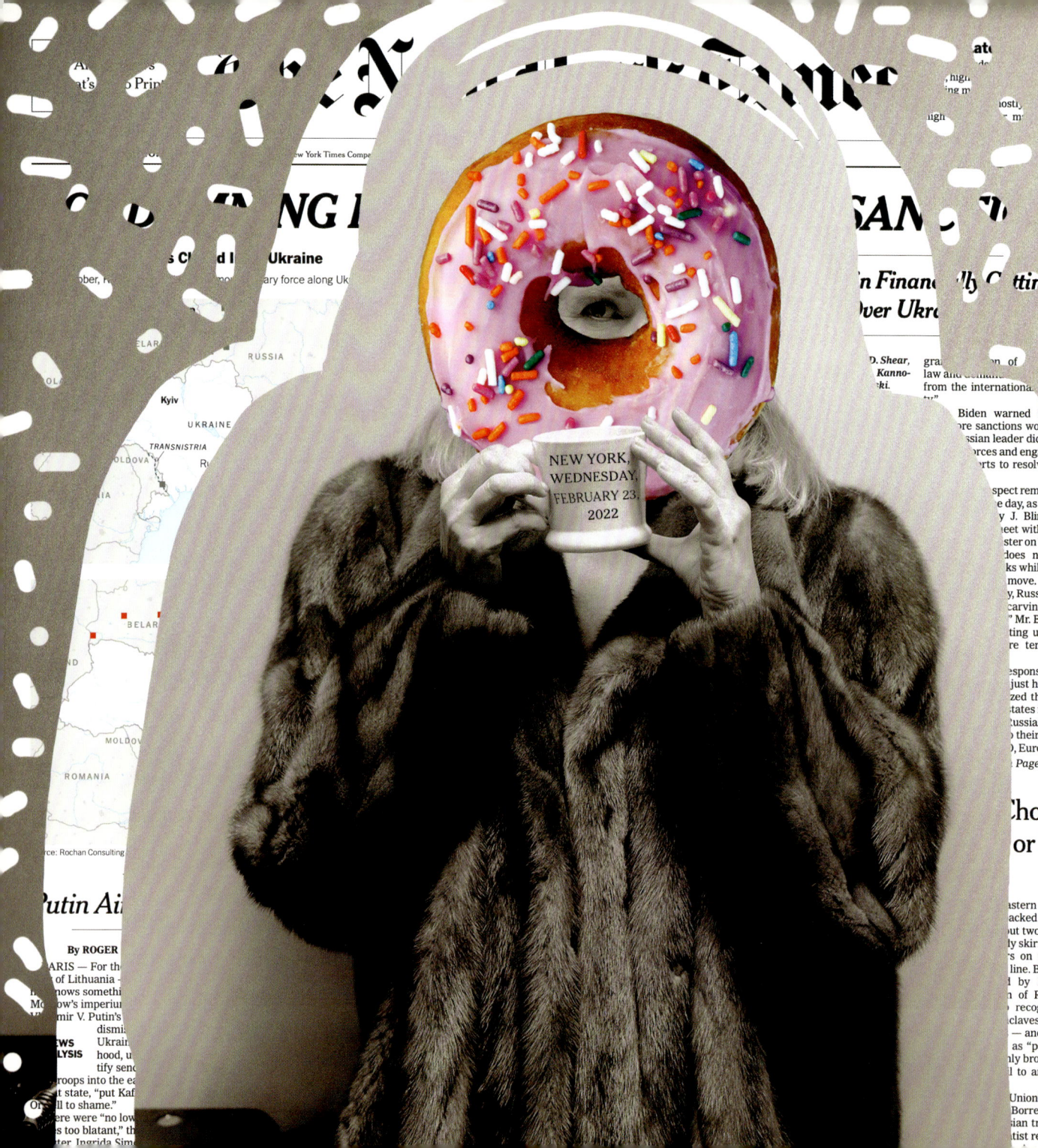

My wife, Stephie, starts each year with a forty-day cleanse where she gives up sugar and caffeine and commits to a particular meditation every day. In 2022, I decided my "cleanse" would be to give up the news. It was taking up too much room in my life and not giving anything back. I needed the space to listen more deeply, to see with more clarity, and to have room to allow my thoughts to wander with less fear.

Stephie came up with the idea during the cleanse to create a series of forty collages using the front page of the newspaper and my images to obscure the news. She'd work late into the night, after our boys were asleep, wrestling the day's news into submission. I love the resulting series, which she called *Newsbreak*.

Working with Stephie is the most fun of all. When we create something together, it always brings out the best in both of us. I like to think our relationship is fed by going to sleep every night laughing. Why is it so funny when the lights go out next to someone you love?

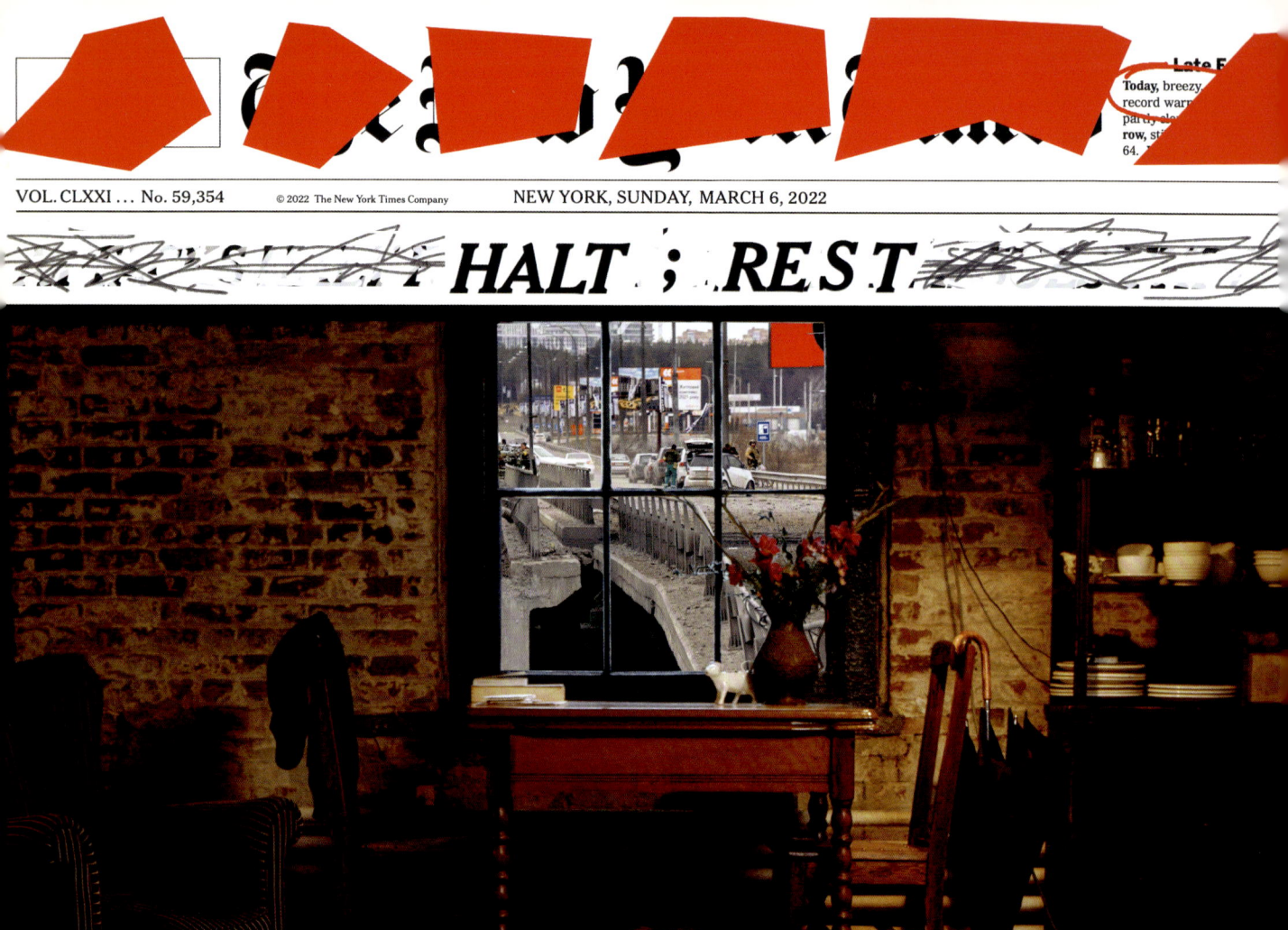

VOL. CLXXI ... No. 59,354   © 2022 The New York Times Company   NEW YORK, SUNDAY, MARCH 6, 2022

Late E

Today, breezy
record warm
partly cle
row, st
64.

HALT ; REST

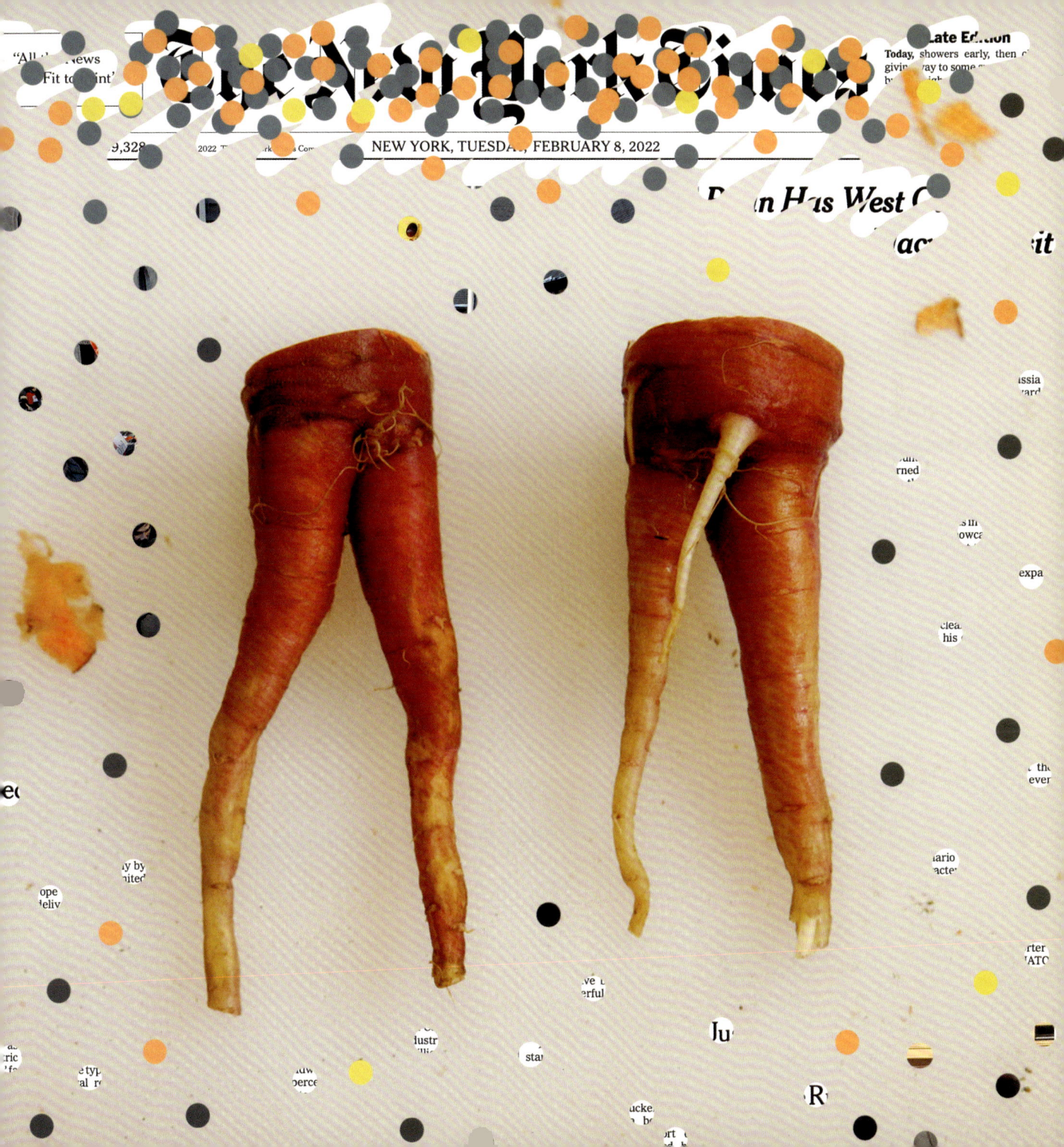

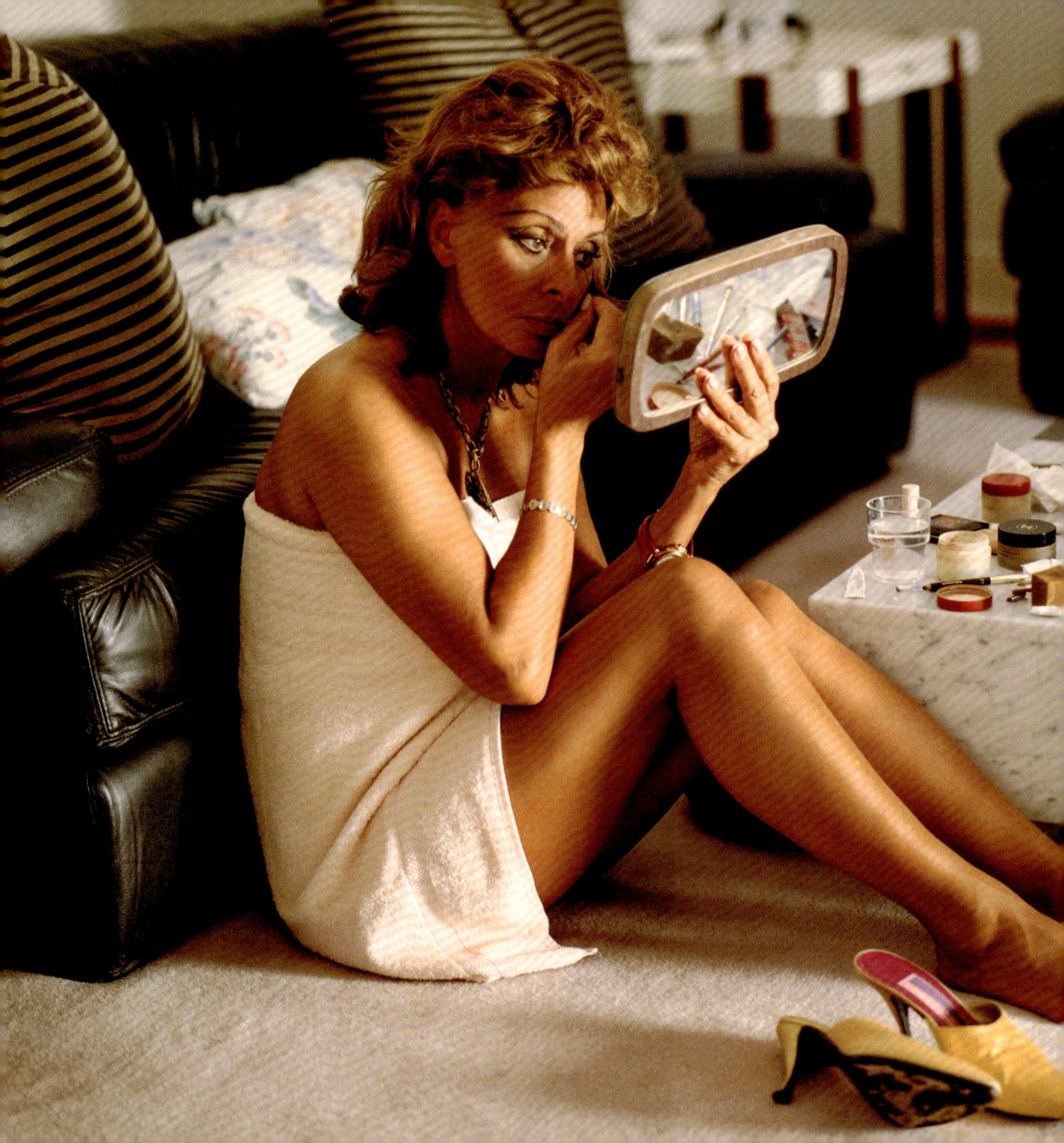

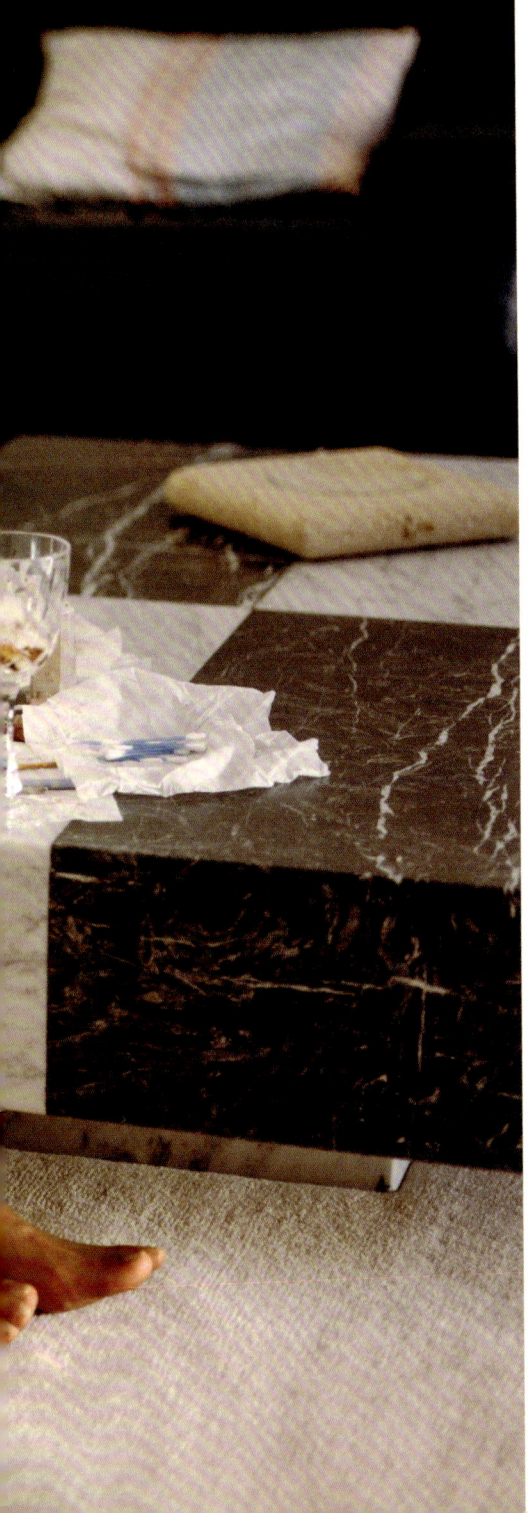

I found an Italian villa in Beverly Hills to shoot Sophia Loren for *Allure*. She walked in alone, no support team, wrapped herself in a towel, grabbed a glass of wine, and sat down. She did her own makeup and put on this great Todd Oldham dress. She then agreed to strap on a leaf blower and go around the garden—a more elegant and lovely actress I have never met.

We had a grand feast after the shoot, linen napkins and all. When she did her lips after lunch, she pressed them to a napkin, making a perfect imprint. I had her sign it—the only autograph I have ever asked for my in entire career.

My time with subjects is often incredibly brief. A small window into a life I would never get to share without my camera. Kate Spade was just incredibly fun. Painting her toenails at her desk was not on the agenda, but it became one of my favorite shots ever. How do you get that shot? You just ask, then climb up on something to get a good angle. The rest of the shoot was equally sweet, full of color and life.

When I read about sadness in someone that I shot's life, I wonder, *Am I blind to the dark side?* Maybe in my pictures. But in every life, even lives with incredible sadness, there is also joy.

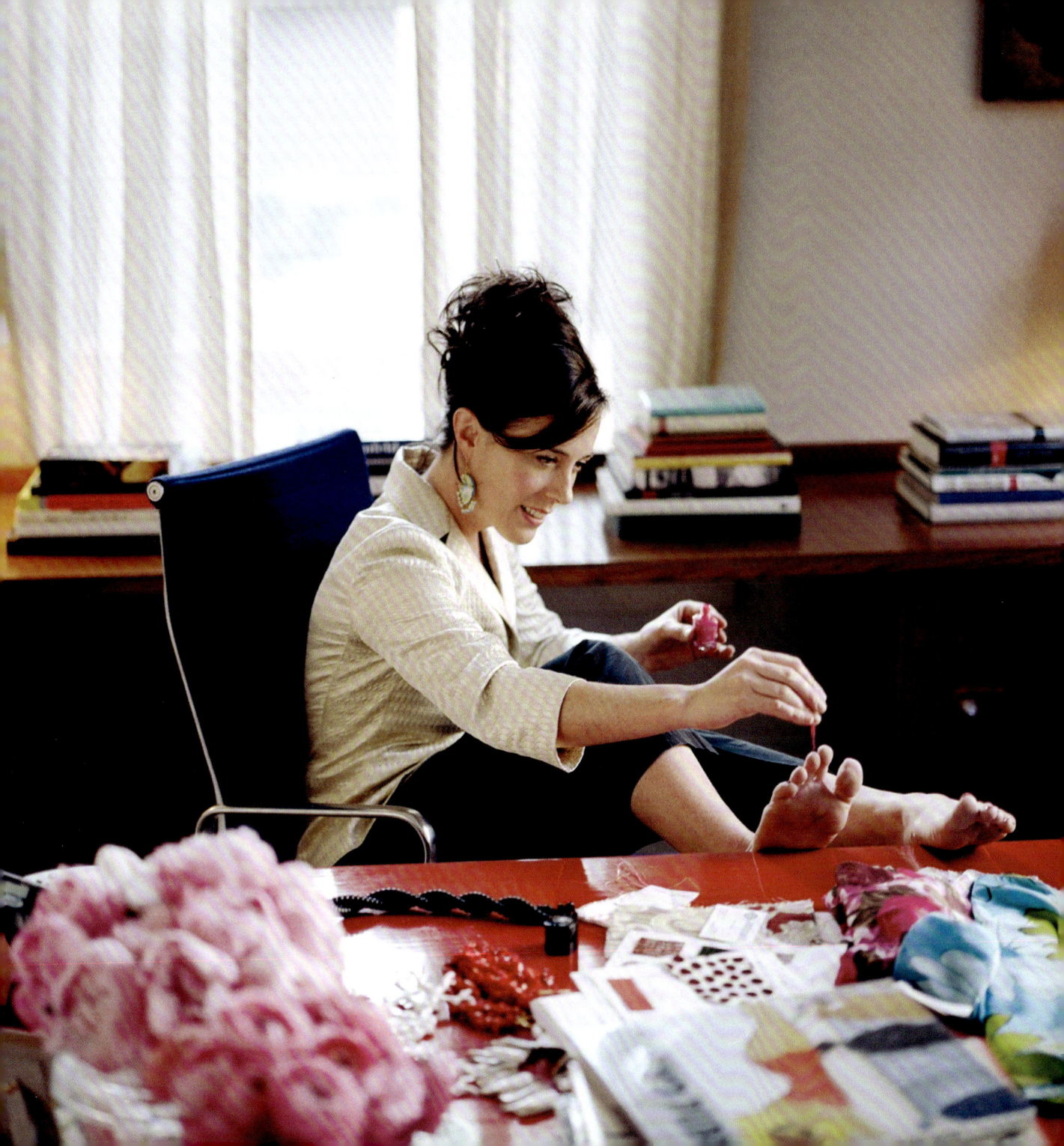

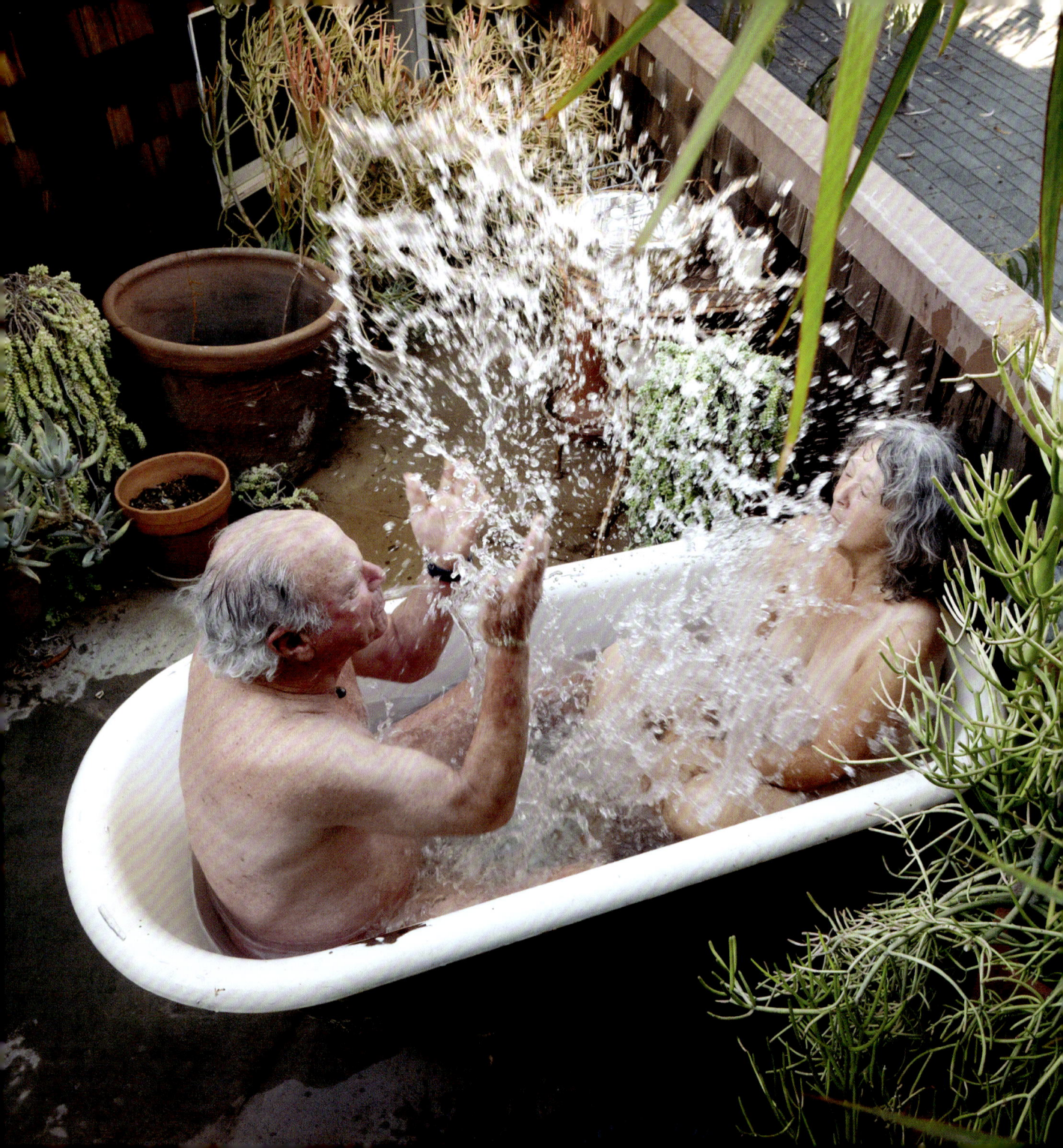

Sometimes I look at the wall of framed images in my studio and think how incredible it is that no one ever ages. Aunt Kay and Uncle John never stop kissing. Mac Miller is always in ecstasy, playing to his audience.

In photos, friends and family are together and having fun in perpetuity. When the subjects are alive, it conveys one thing. When they are gone, the photos take on whole other meanings. Like Duane Michals has written on the bottom of one of his photos, "This photograph is my proof. There was that afternoon . . . She embraced me, and we were so happy. It did happen, she did love me. Look, see for yourself."

When I am taking photos, I am totally aware of the moment. But I'm not thinking about the legacy or life a photo will have or how the meaning will change through the years. If my pictures are about joy, how do they fit or feel in a world where people will inevitably face sadness? When I photographed my friend Andy Clark holding a burning piece of wood,

IT FELT LIKE HE WAS ILLUMINATING HIMSELF WITH A BEAUTIFUL, DANGEROUS GLOW.

After his tragic death, the whole meaning changed. Now I treasure this portrait for completely different reasons.

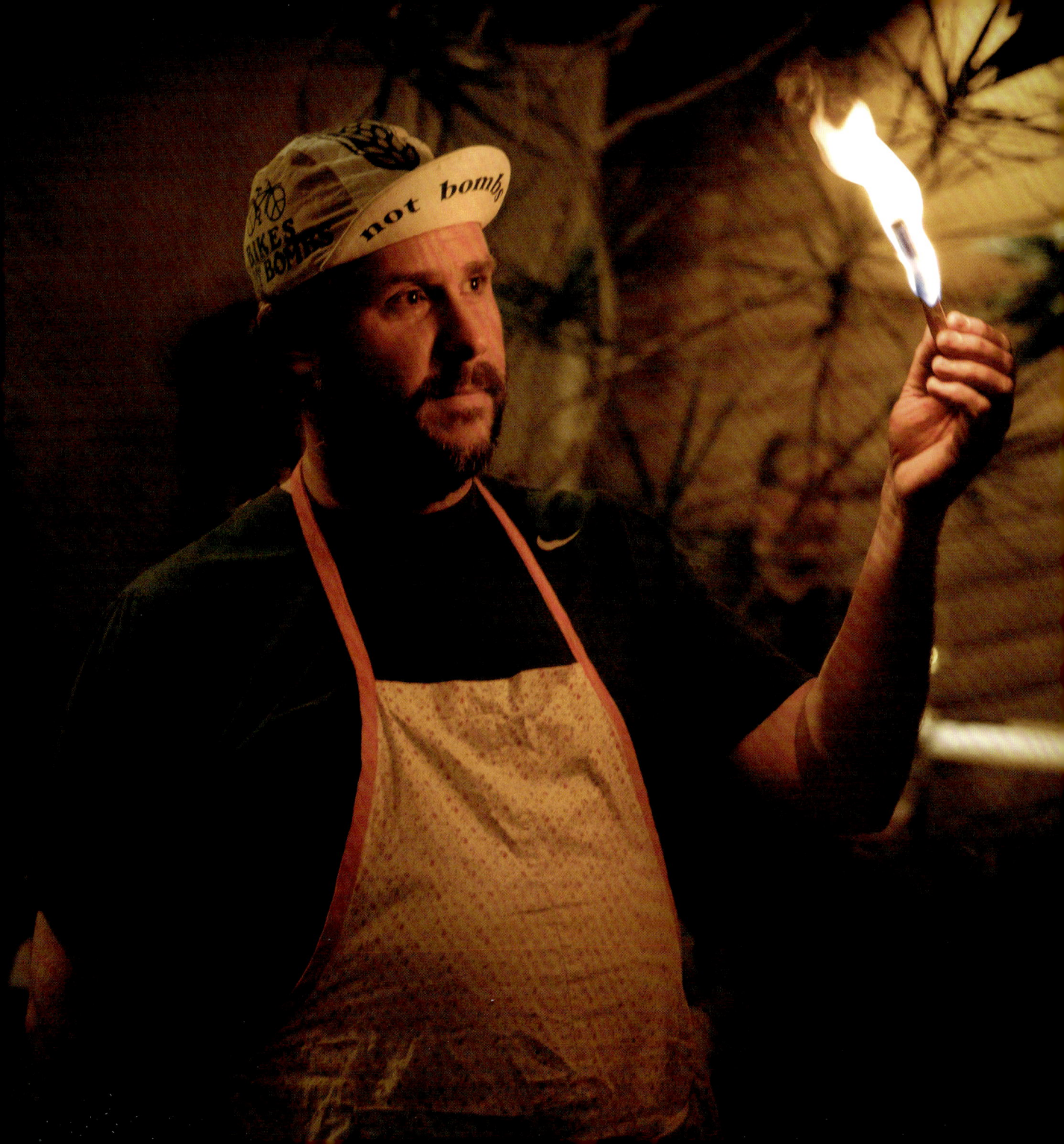

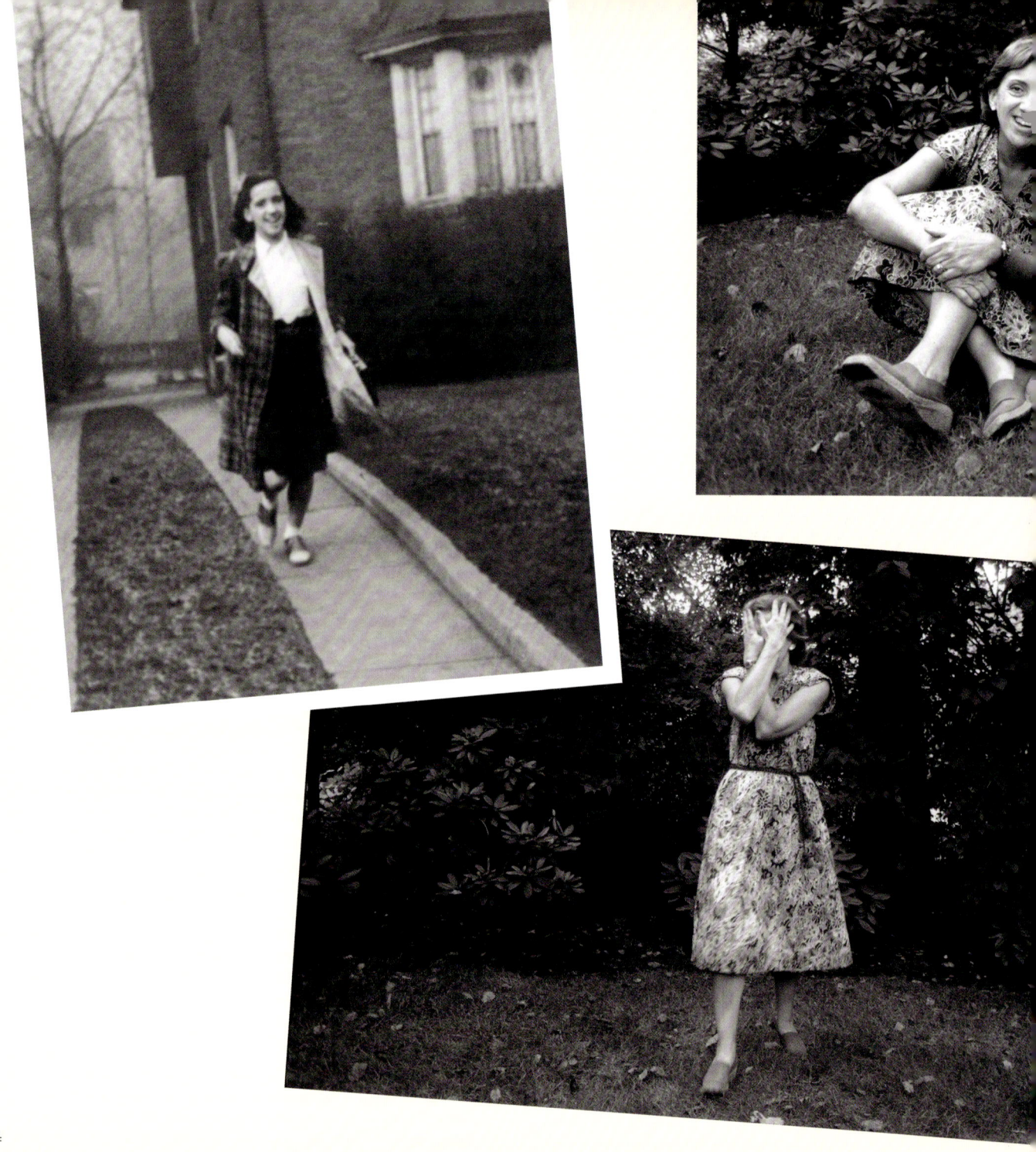

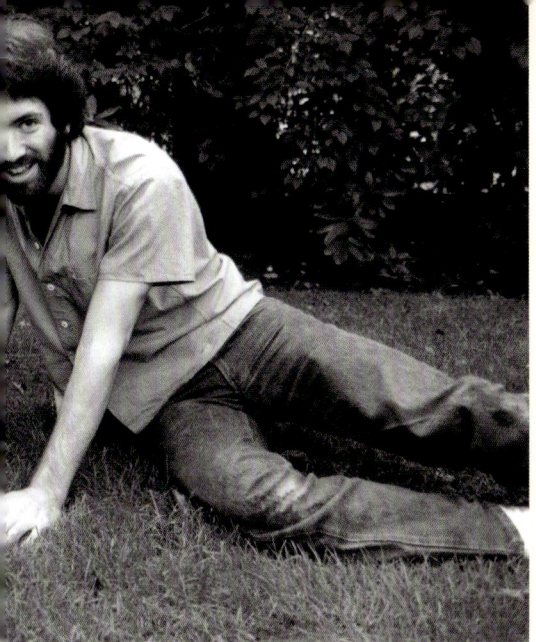
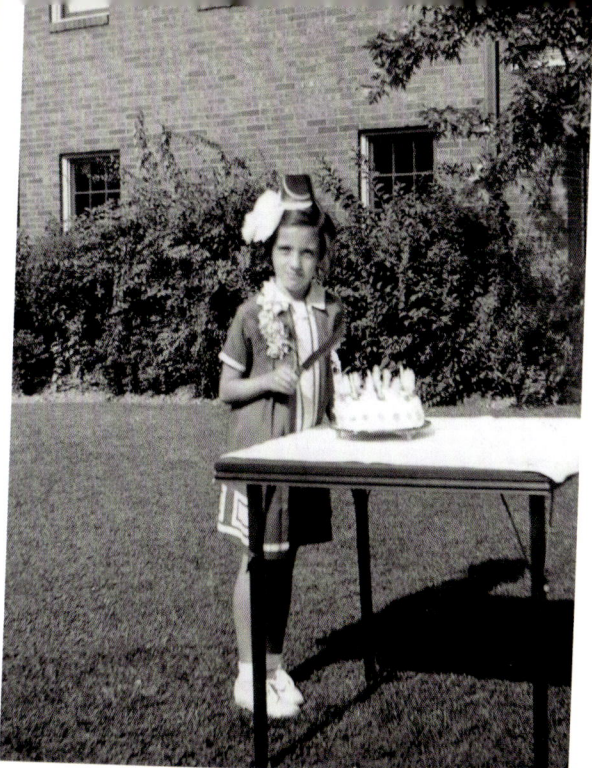

My mother is still alive in the way we move and think and live our lives and mostly, in the way we love. She is alive in how my son Jackson says "thank you," looks people in the eye, and makes them feel special. She is alive in Asher's ability to wake up so energetic each day and to go out into the world with such abandon and confidence. She is alive in the way my wife, Stephie, reminds us to always keep the kitchen clean in case a friend surprises us at the back door.

If I believed that when you die everything you are just stops being, that would be too sad to imagine. When I look around at those I hold so close, I know we are the sum of generations of love.

My parents raised me to be curious and to be on a lifelong search for how we are all connected. My father was Jewish and worked in a community an hour away from our home that had few, if any, Jews. My father believed that people who didn't like him just didn't know him. Bankers, businesspeople, restaurant owners—everyone he came in contact with could not help but eventually come to love Jack Lange.

My dad worked six days a week, and on the seventh day we went to Pittsburgh Steelers games. He had six tickets and two rules: whomever he took to the games never paid for the tickets (he wasn't rich, but he was generous), and we never left before the final play. I would sit right next to him, often freezing cold, wondering if the coffee or the cigar was keeping him warm.

While the Steelers were sometimes horrible and occasionally immaculate, he always loved the games. But what he cherished more was sharing the games with a whole crew of friends.

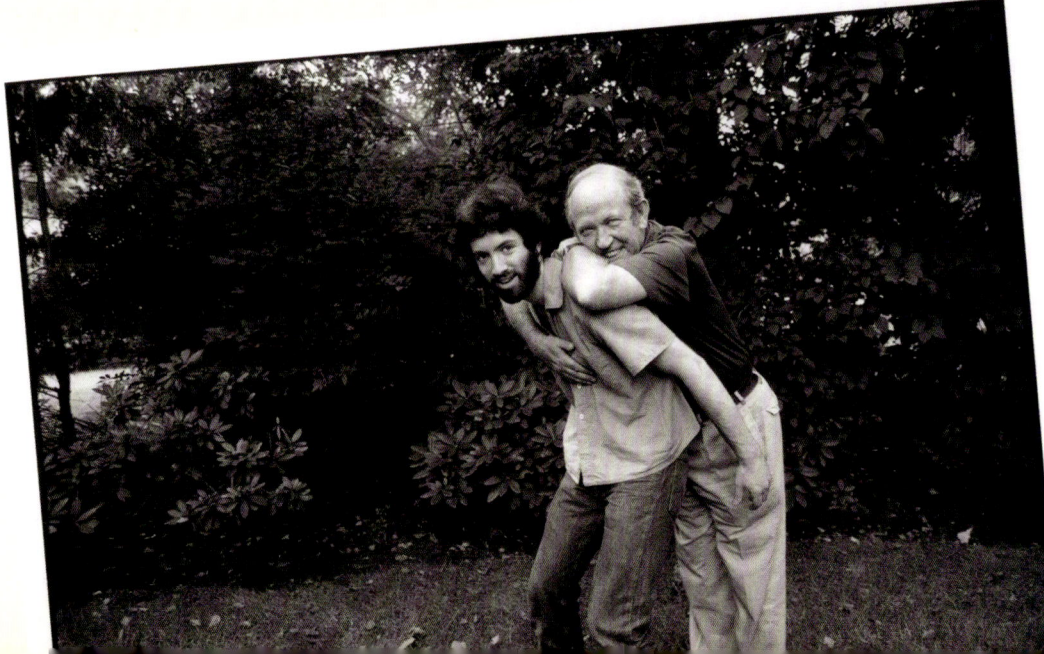

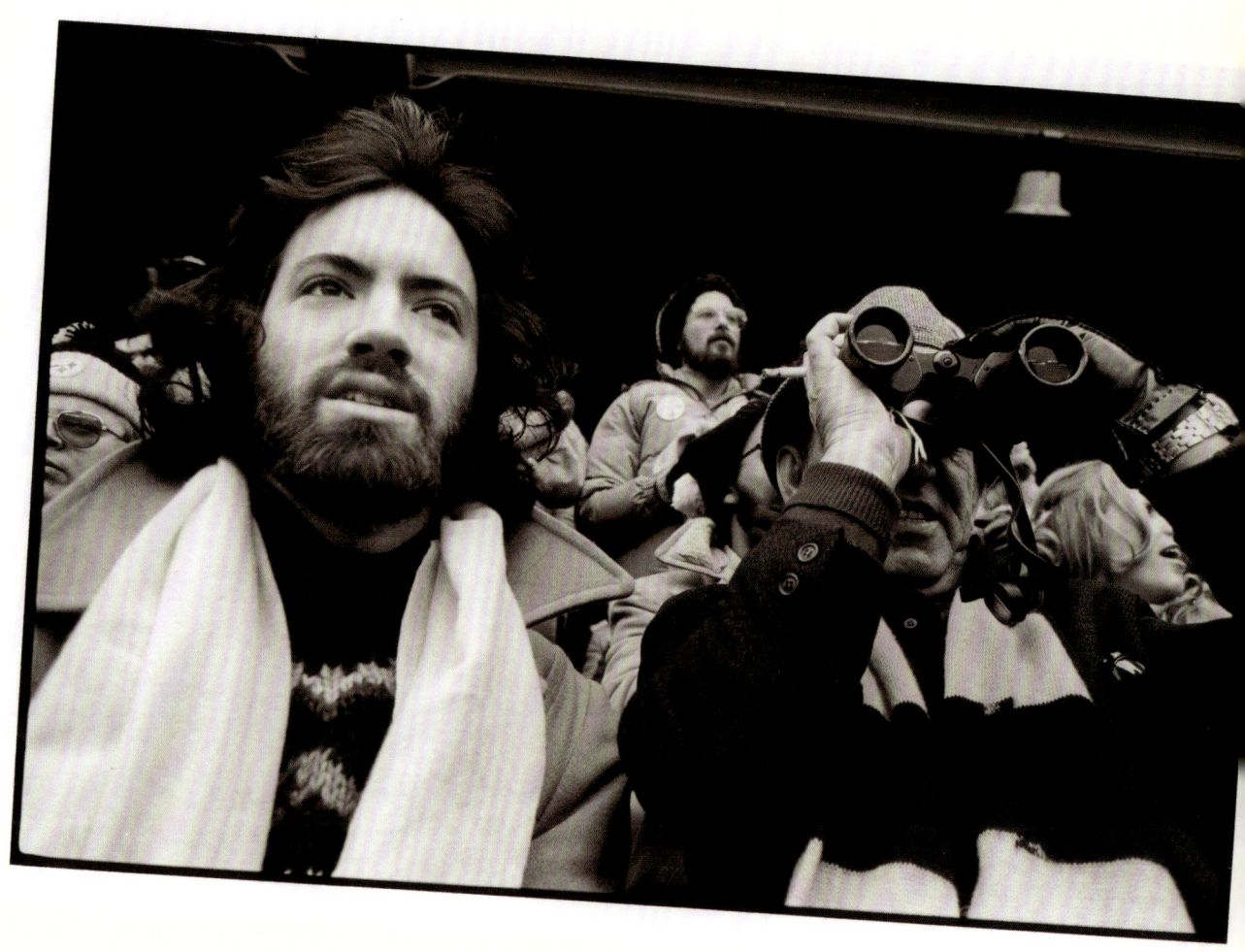

THE REAL JOY WAS NOT WATCHING THE
   STEELERS ON THE FIELD AS MUCH AS THE
RITUAL OF ALL BEING TOGETHER.

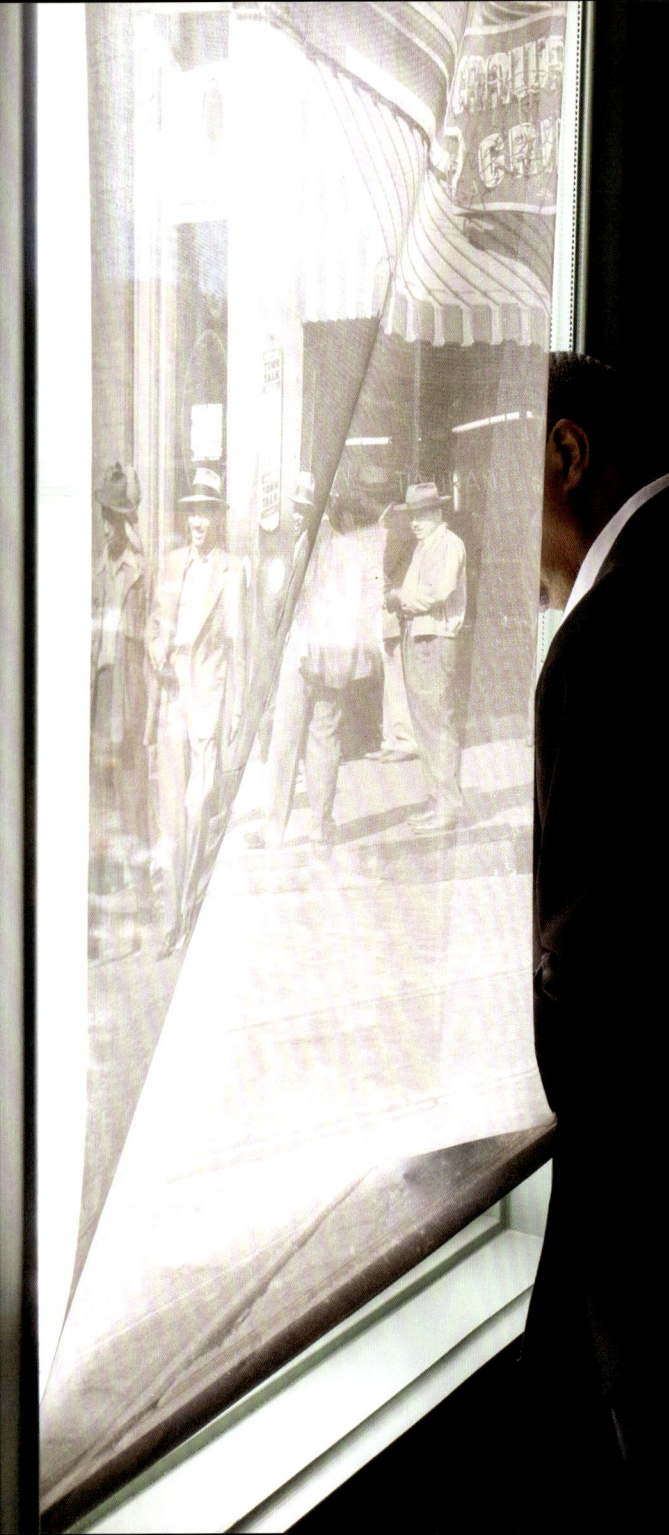

Pittsburgh is the childhood home of the famed playwright August Wilson. Millions of dollars were raised to refurbish and rededicate his family's Hill District home as a museum, educational space, and outdoor theater. I was brought in to take portraits at the opening, and I set up in the home's original kitchen.

The first thing I noticed was the sunlight filtering in through the cotton shades from the north and east. That was the same exact light that August Wilson's family had experienced when cooking and eating there. It felt like holy ground. Tapping into the original light felt like the perfect jumping-off place for my portraits. Seeing Pittsburgh mayor Ed Gainey looking out the window felt like the past connecting with the future in front of my lens.

One summer, at a beach house, my son Jackson ran up the stairs, yelling, "Dad, grab your camera. You have to see the light in my room!" Jackson is a photographer's son, after all, so I ran back down the steps with him.

"Dad! Look at my bed. The sunset is on my bed!" And it was true—the light from the sunset had turned his bed pink and orange.

"Look! The sunset is on my wall!" His bright-white walls were now warm pink.

"Dad! The sunset is on me!" And I took that picture, too.

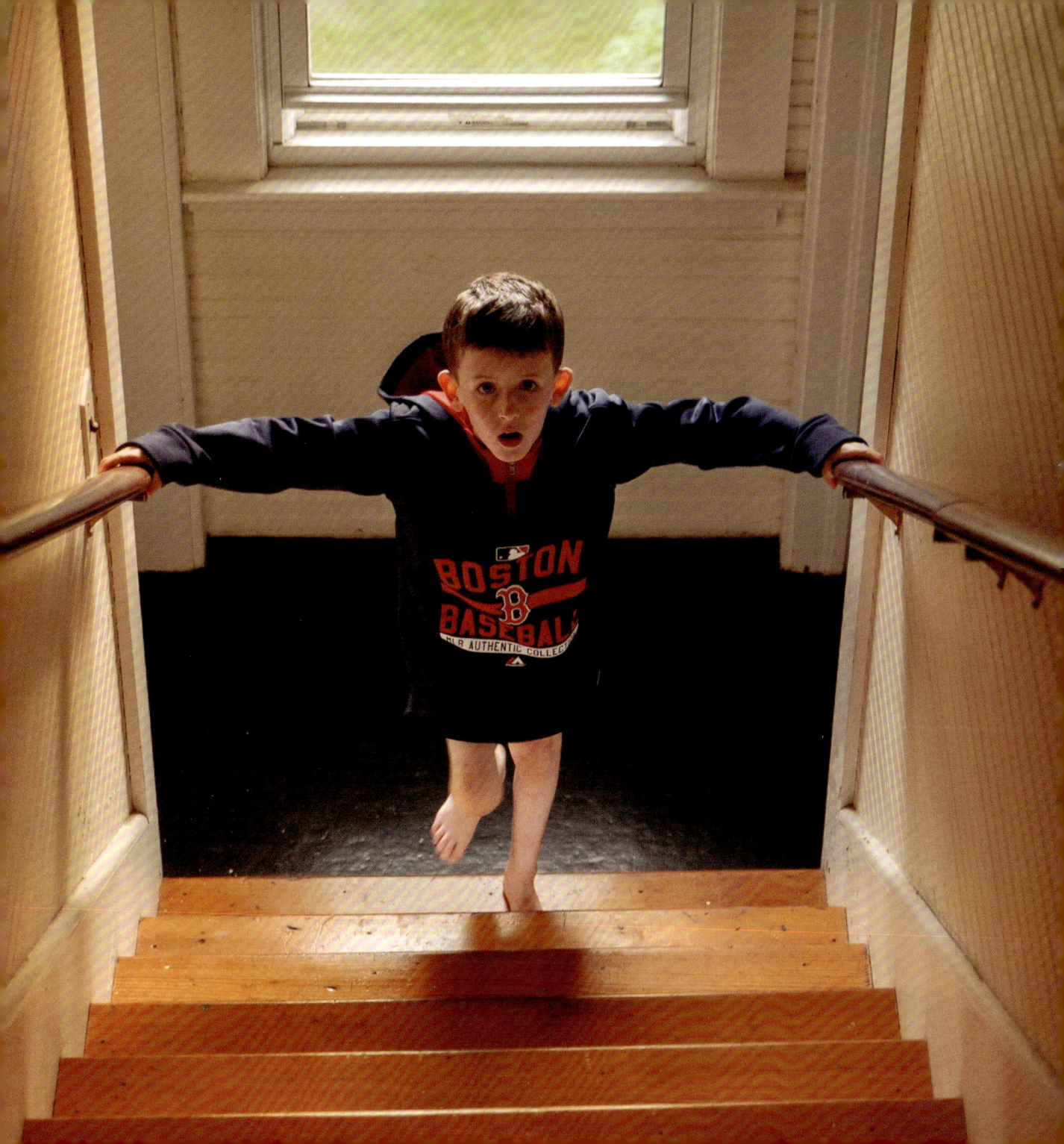

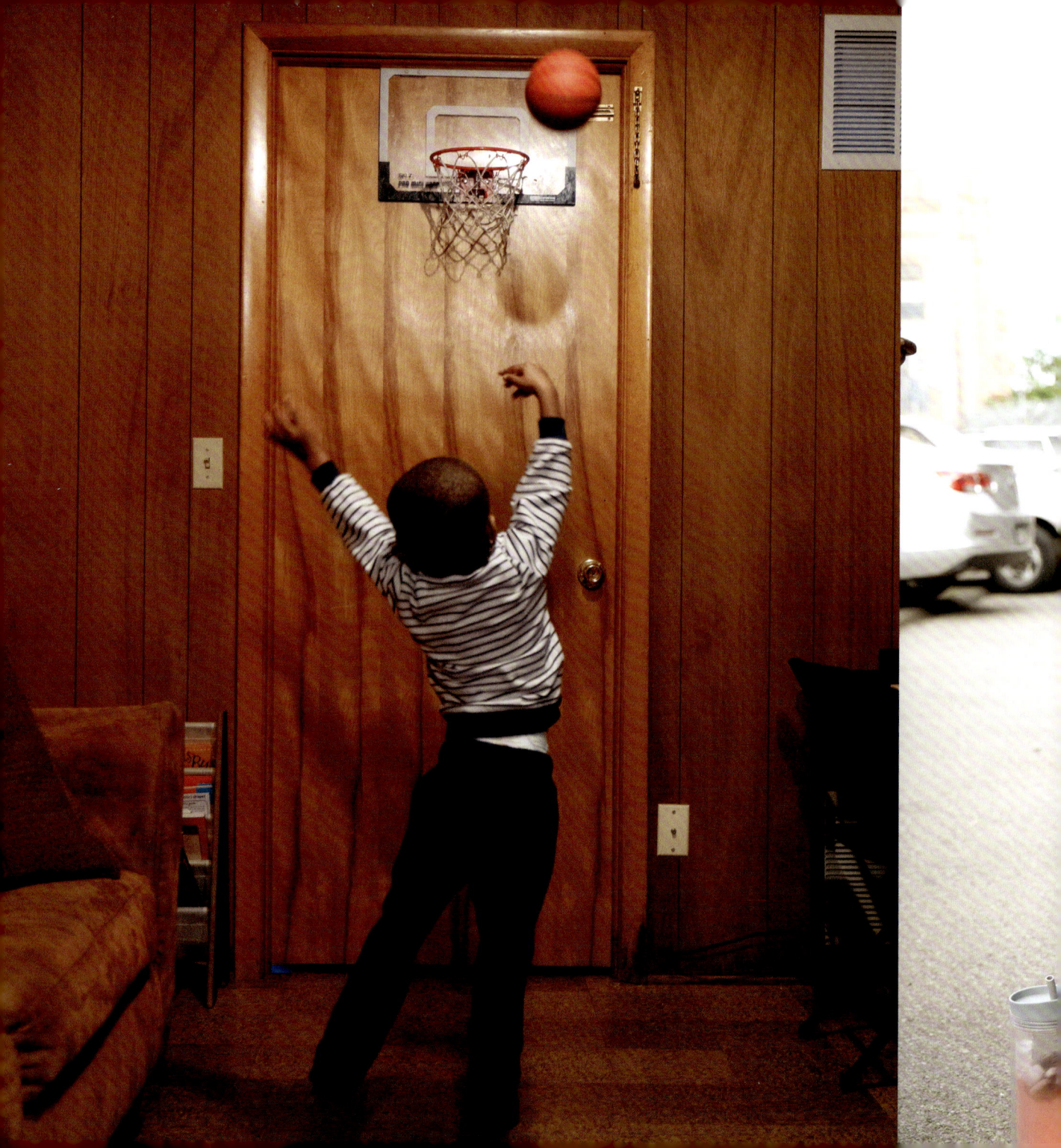

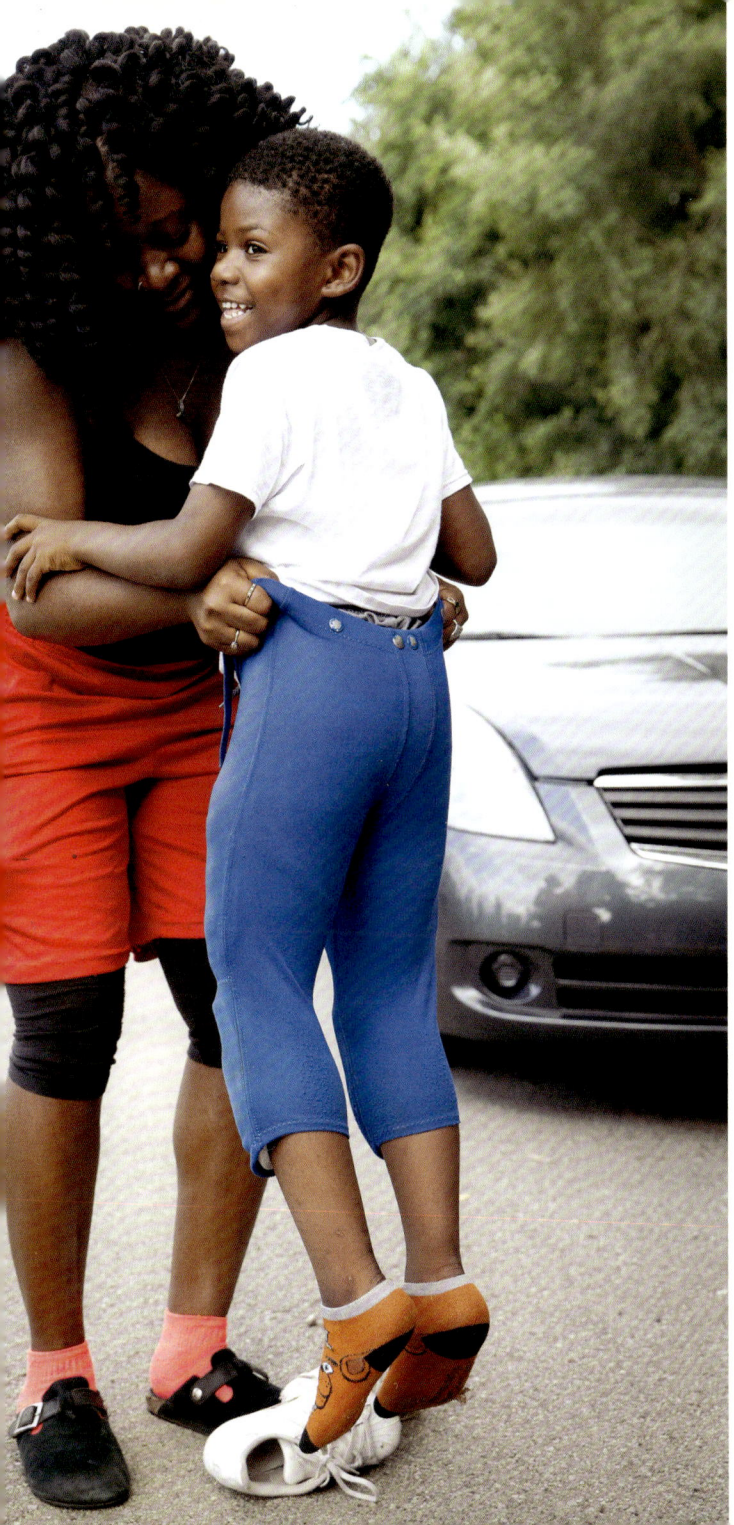

Dick's Sporting Goods hired me, but they didn't want action shots. They weren't interested in photographs of a new brand of clothes or equipment. They wanted me to capture the emotional side of youth sports— what it felt like to play. It was a dream job that left me open to explore anything I wanted.

I got to shoot the loud moments and the quiet ones: the insides of packed cars, the motel rooms, the loading and unloading of equipment early in the morning and late at night. I recorded team dugouts and the taking off of cleats after a long tournament. These small gestures often reveal the moments of greatest passion. They are not about winning or losing, but about being.

The Pittsburgh Symphony
Orchestra (PSO) had guidelines
around their photography. The
musicians had to be shot against
a dark modeled canvas custom
painted in Italy, and I had to use
the classic lighting style that they
had established for their "look."
I began with their youngest
member, twenty-two-year-old
violist Sean Juhl, who later
posted about his experience:

"I initially thought that the shoot
would be formal and joyless—that
I would show up, take a few static
shots, and be out of there in fifteen
minutes. After an hour had flown
by, though, I knew that this was
one of the most interesting and
fun photographic experiences
of my life. George had a way with
words that lightened the mood
right away, and instead of sitting
through some stuffy, tedious
process, I really got to witness
a fellow artist at work."

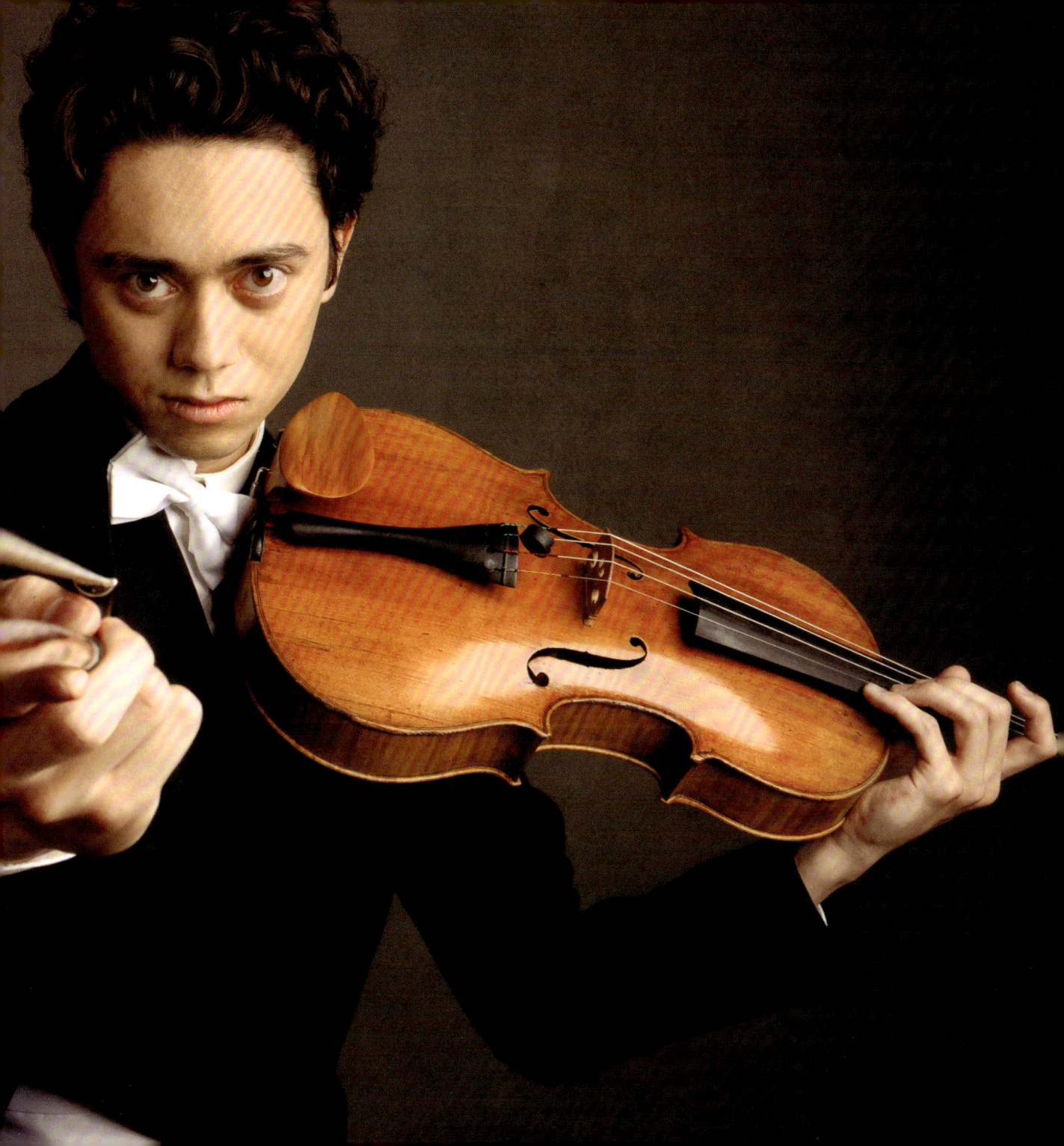

When I was five or six years old, my mother bought me a recording of Beethoven's Symphony No. 1 by the Pittsburgh Symphony Orchestra. I listened to it over and over (and over), holding the album cover in my hands. On the back cover was a black-and-white photo of the orchestra and a very serious portrait of the conductor, William Steinberg, with the credit: *Photo by Ben Spiegel.*

Who was Ben Spiegel?

It seemed to me, even then, that it must be wild to have the entire orchestra posing for your camera. I learned later that Ben was a bassoonist in the PSO who loved photography. He eventually put down his bassoon and became the official photographer for the orchestra, traveling all over the world with them and documenting their journeys.

I never met Ben but I read that he said, "Music is a wonderful discipline for any profession. You learn to listen, look, and anticipate, and that's what photography is, too."

When I later stood in front of the Dress Circle in Heinz Hall with the entire PSO posing onstage for my camera, I thought about Ben Spiegel and that recording of Beethoven's Symphony No. 1 that my mom put in my hands all those years ago. I needed to connect with the eighty musicians before me, so I ran down to the stage and shared that story.

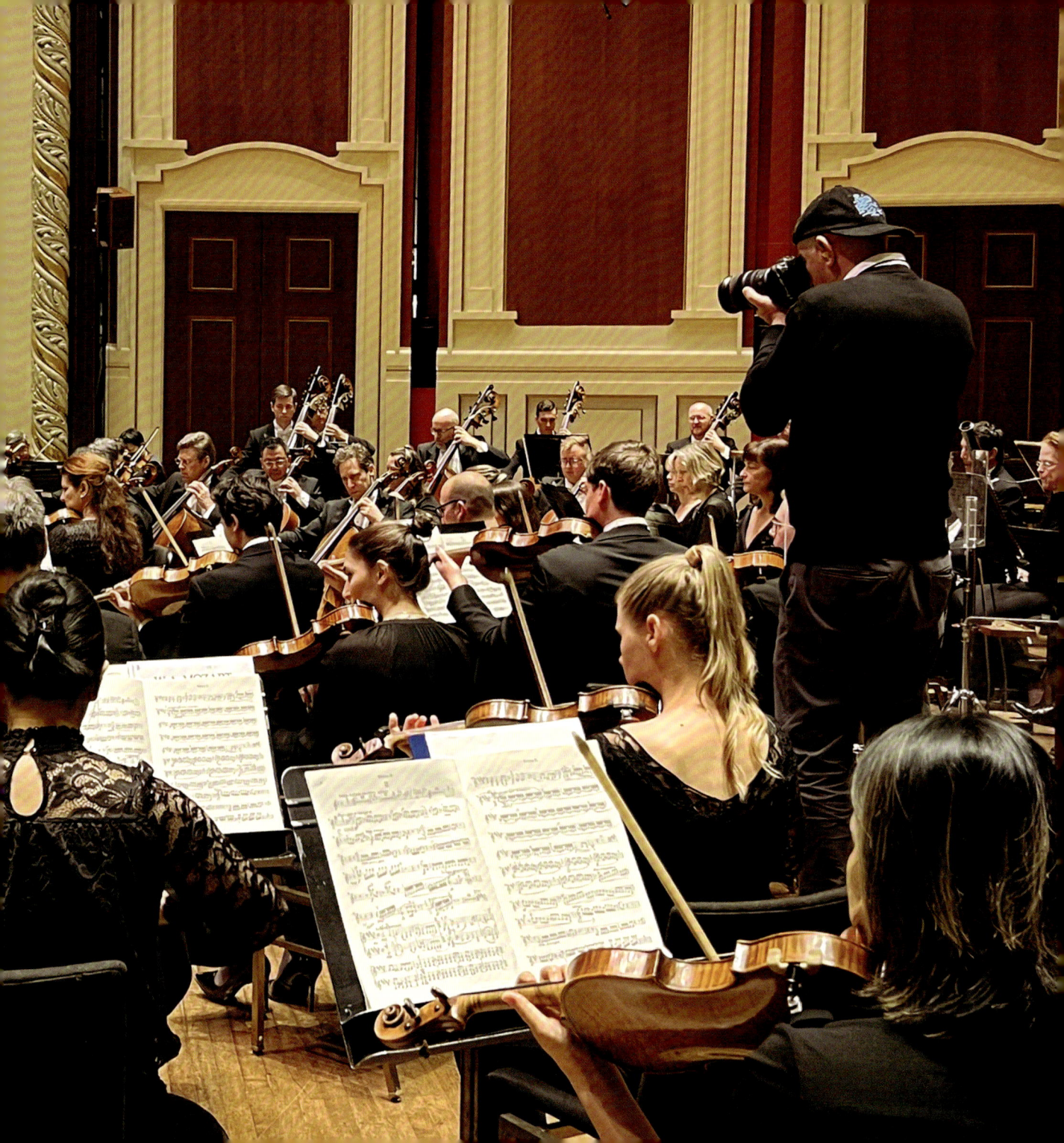

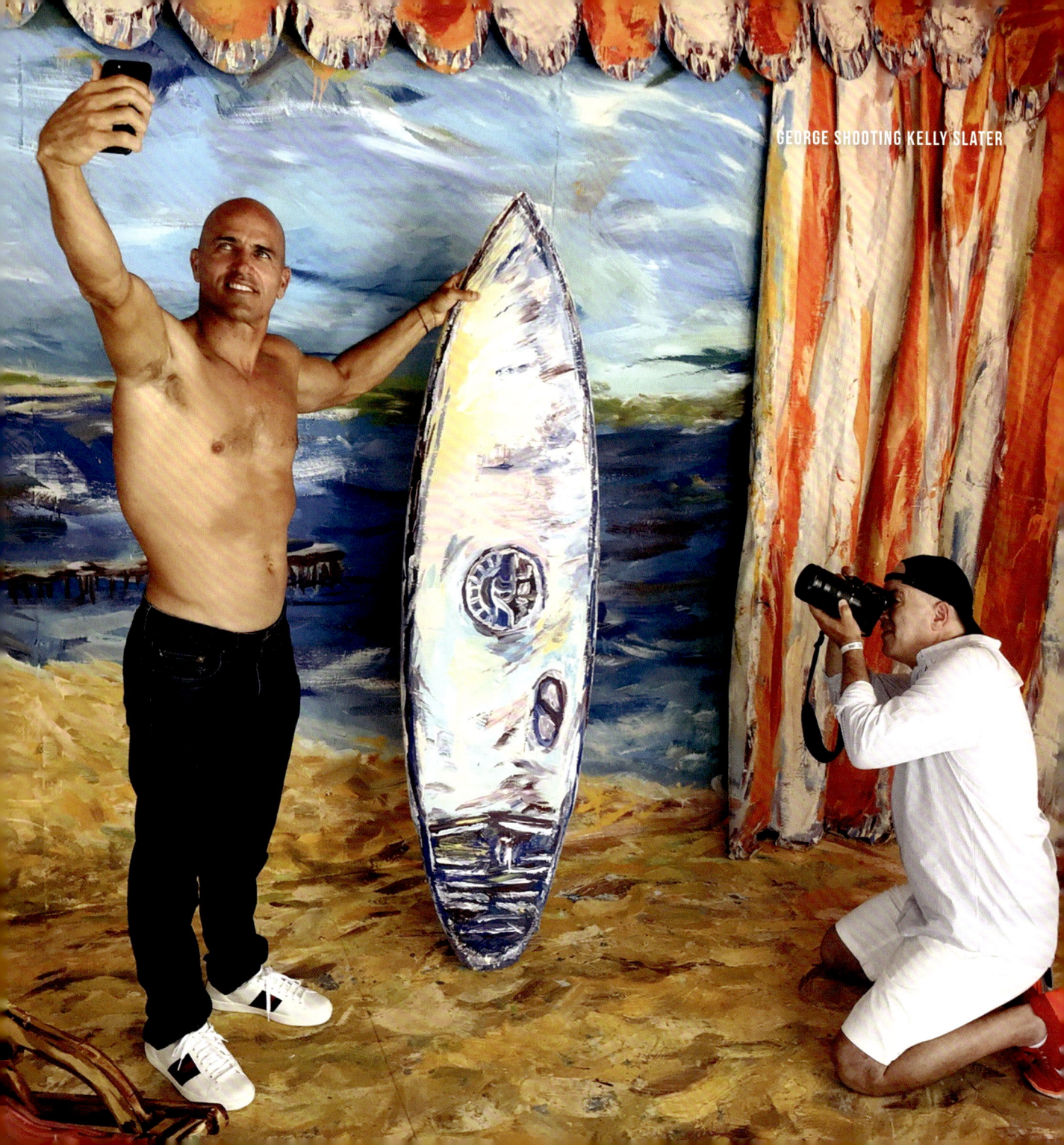

GEORGE SHOOTING KELLY SLATER

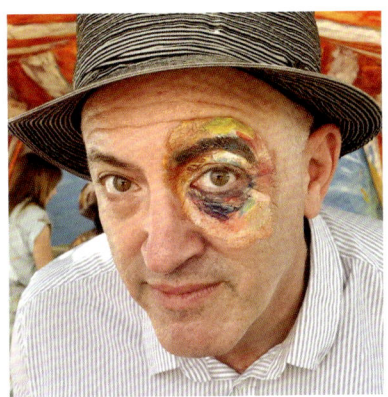

LA painter Alexa Meade decorated a set for Instagram at Cannes Lions, the festival of creativity for the international creative marketing community. She painted it in her colorful, impressionistic style, where subjects and props are meant to blend in to the background.

On my second day, I asked a subject to take a painted wooden apple and a paddle and smack the apple at my camera that was over fifteen feet away. What I didn't imagine was the apple flying right at my left eye. An hour later I was at the hospital in Cannes.

The next day, Alexa gave my black eye her impressionist touch, and my bruise disappeared.

When I get to photograph true creatives, it is a different kind of party. When George Lois became the creative director of *Esquire* magazine, he took over the cover decision–making process and made it his own. He insisted on total control. Ninety-two covers later, his brashness, his rebellion, and his sheer genius changed the medium forever.

Our shoot together was like water-skiing behind a speedboat. Everything that started one way became something else. His case of African masks became a playground—for both of us. His sculpture on the balcony, a muse for his pleasure and naughtiness.

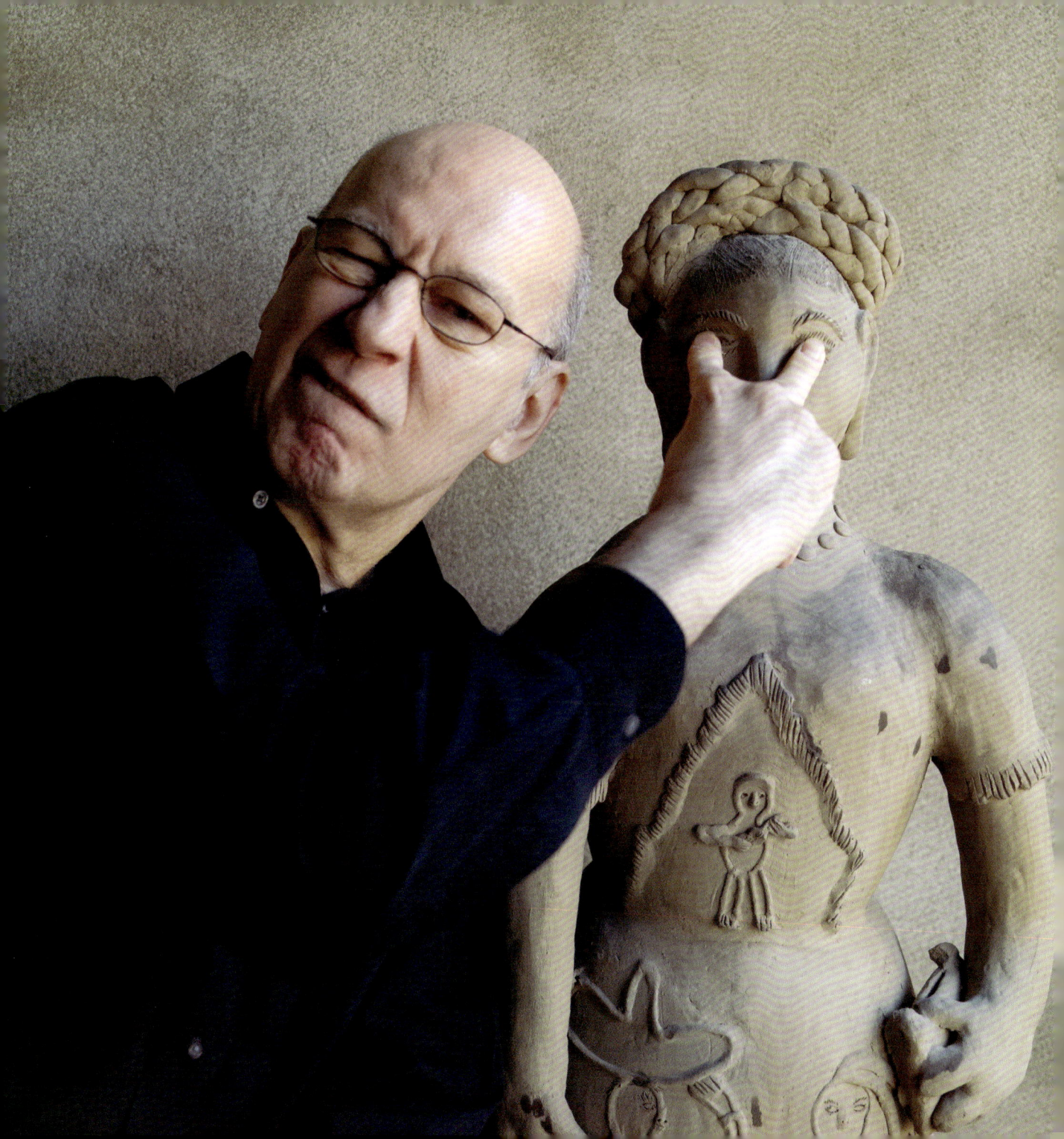

Often, my photos are just a mirror to show people how strong

and beautiful they are. During the COVID-19 pandemic, I worked

on a series with the Pittsburgh Bucks, a youth football team.

Each of these kids shared their strength and beauty with

me in the middle of trying to resurrect a canceled season.

My job was just to share it with the world.

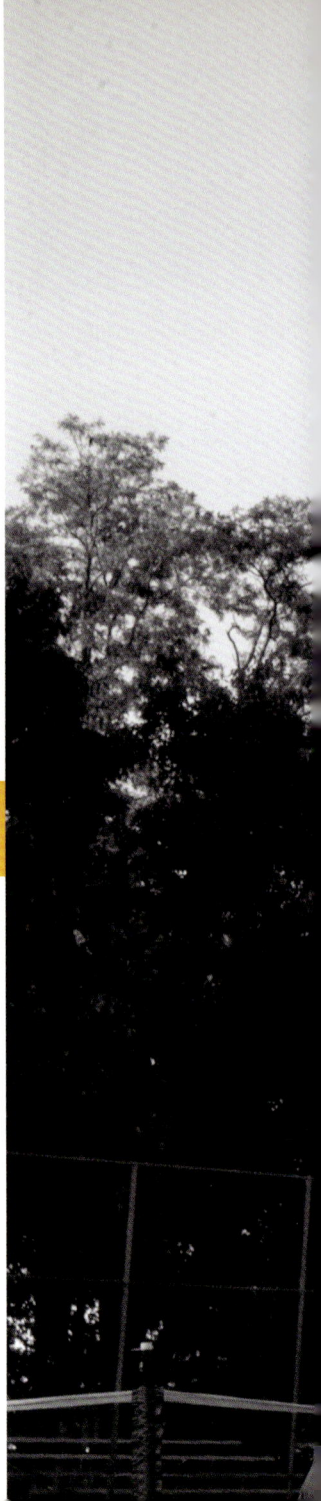

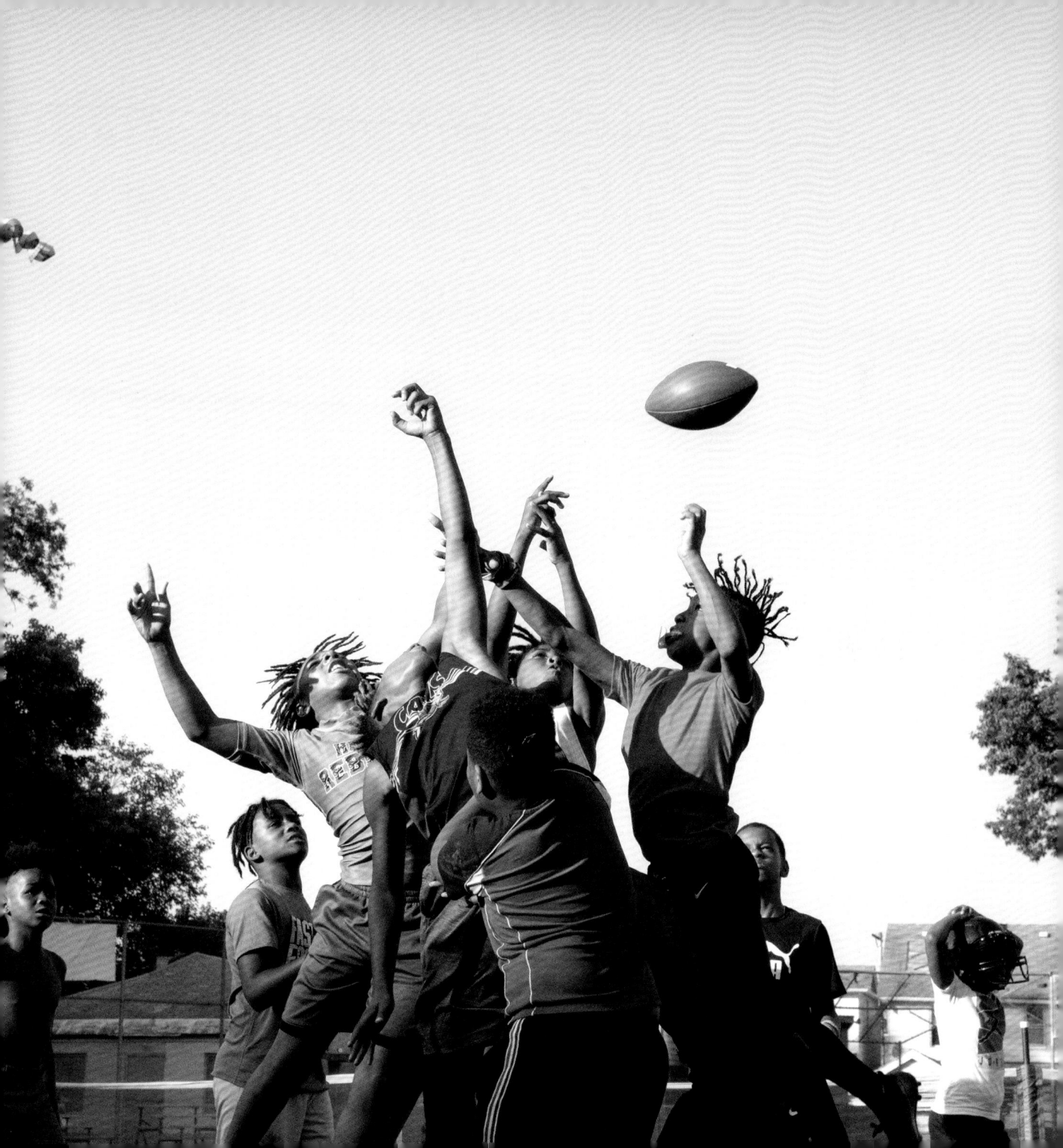

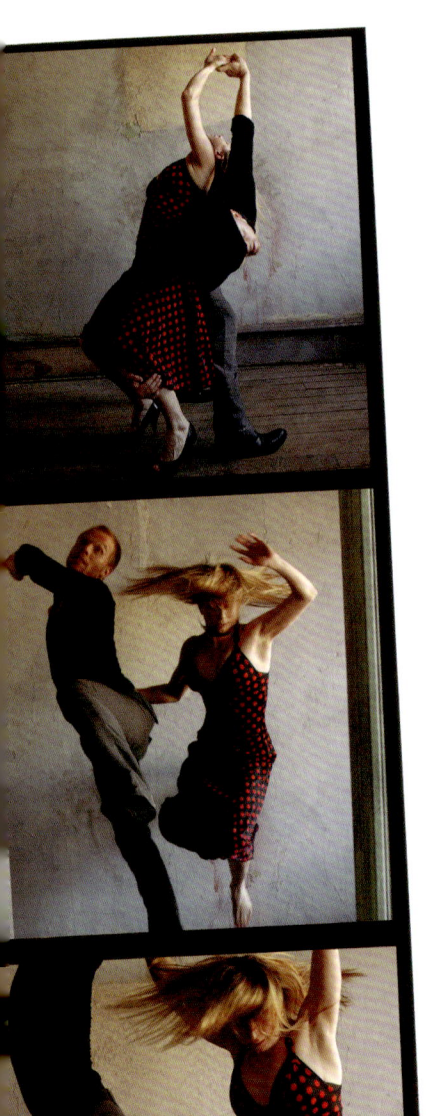

I knew nothing about dance when I met the choreographer Aszure Barton. When she told me I couldn't photograph her company unless I directed them, I panicked. How do I direct world-class dancers? A good start was stealing ideas from Aszure.

Ideas never come from out of nowhere. I am inspired by the smallest details, such as something I saw in the theater, a song I heard, or the smallest movement. Aszure packed every second of her work with so many ideas—even the moments with no movement.

ONCE SHE FREED ME TO DIRECT HER DANCERS, I REALIZED I JUST HAD TO LIGHT A SPARK.

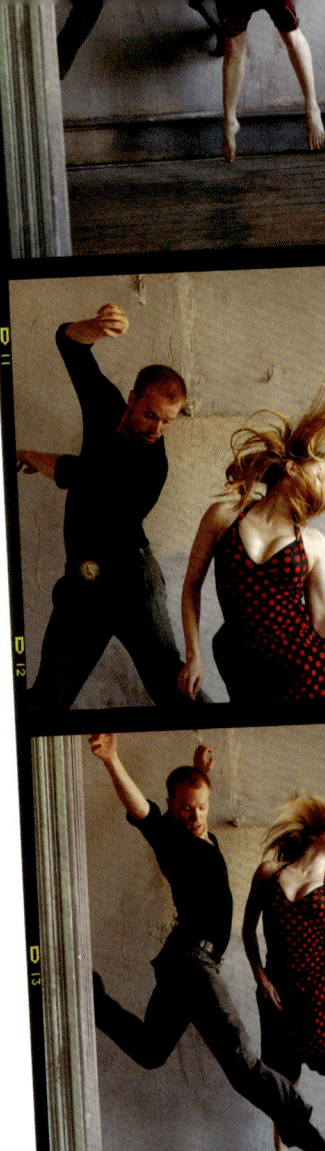

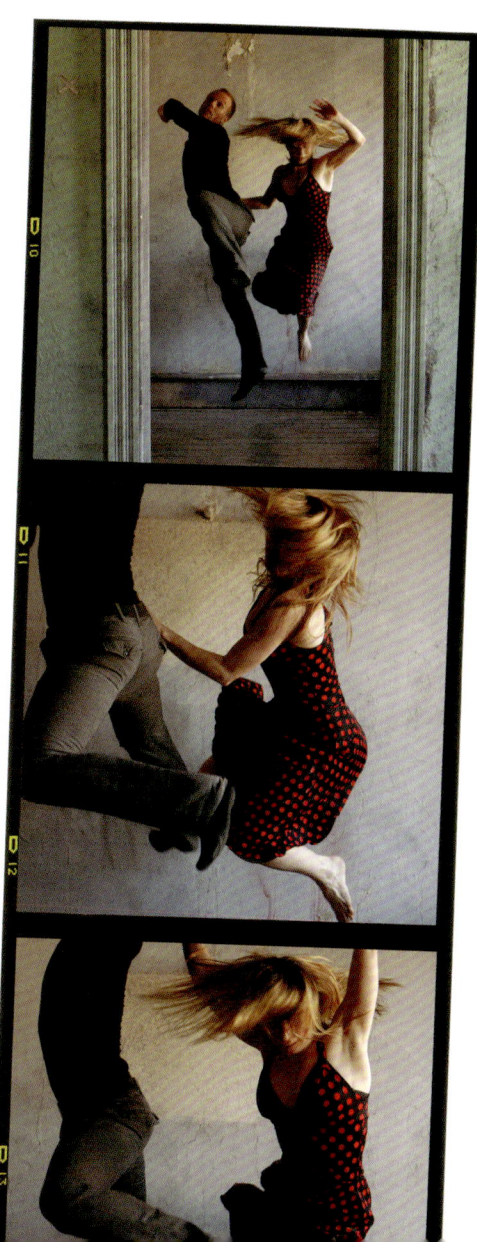
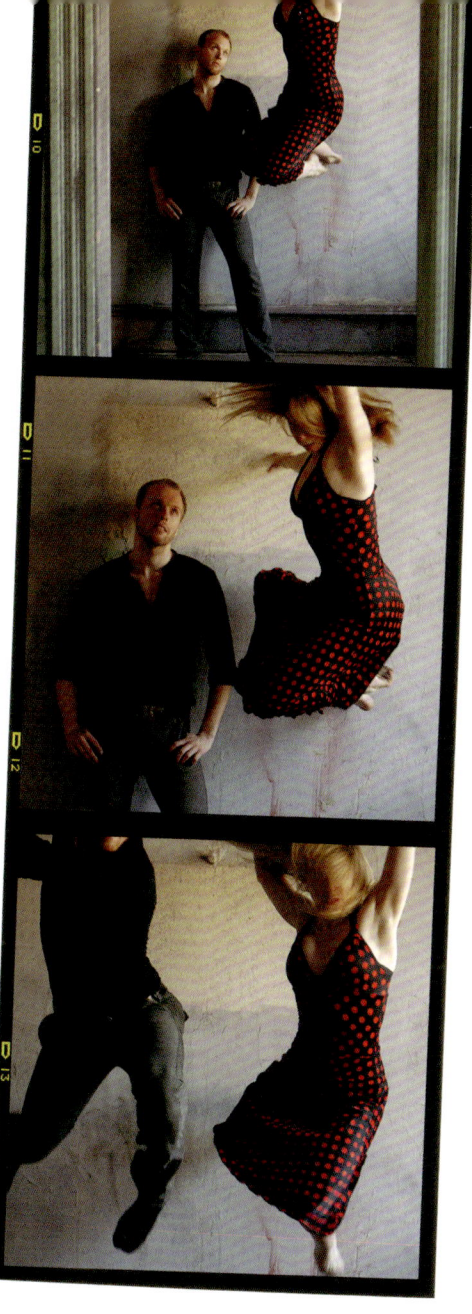

75

In the makeup room, I asked Jim Carrey what his rubbery face was going to look like when he got older. He picked up some clothespins, and we took off from there.

Jim always included kids from the Make-A-Wish Foundation on our many shoots together. That day, a boy wanted to play photographer. Jim agreed and the kid climbed up on an apple box behind my camera. I showed him which button to push. He looked into the camera and the room got quiet. Nervously quiet. Jim stood there for a long while, as the boy kept looking intently into the viewfinder. Suddenly he yells, "GIVE IT TO ME, JIMMY!"

Possibly the single most beautiful moment at any photo shoot in my whole career.

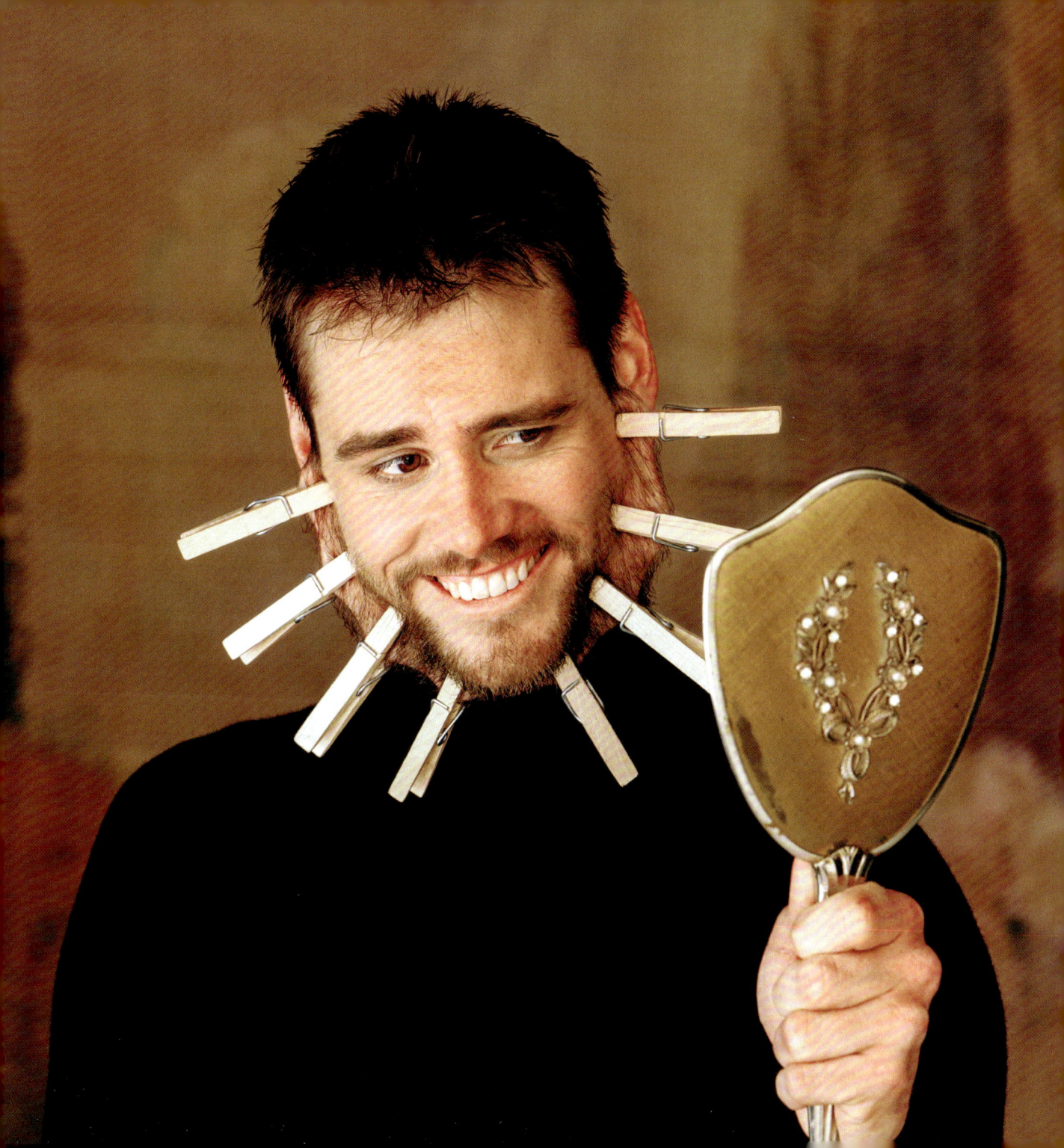

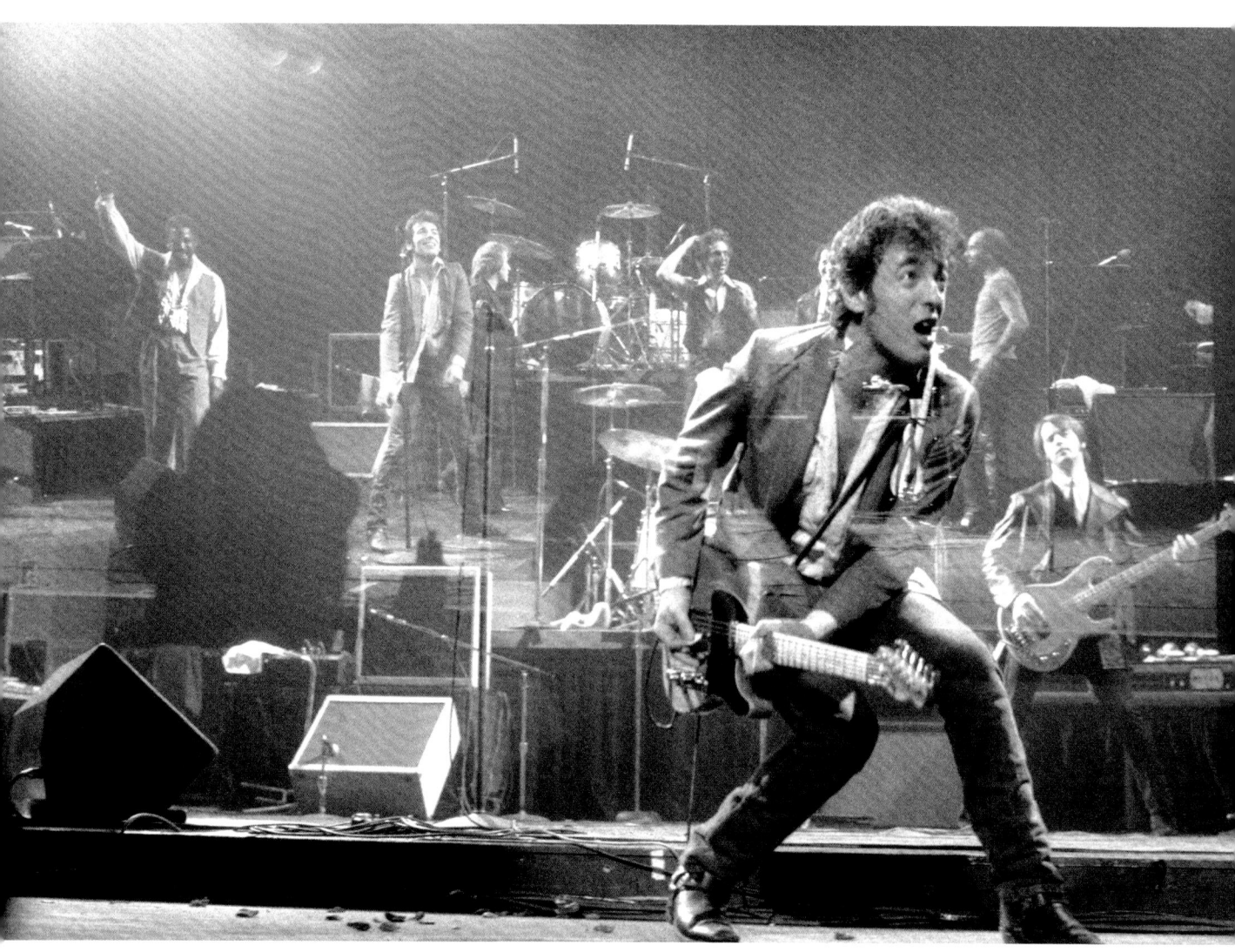

Back in 1978, I went to a Bruce Springsteen concert at the Stanley Theater in Pittsburgh. Of course I snuck my camera in, and I shot from the balcony early in the show. Then I found empty seats in the orchestra close to the stage and accidentally reloaded the camera with that used roll of film.

Initially, I was disappointed at having shot the roll twice and double exposing everything. But time is funny—years later, the double exposures look like magic rather than mistakes. It was a huge revelation seeing the images blown up as fine-art prints years later. There were so many details I had never seen before, especially with the E Street Band twice in every frame. It just took a little time and distance for the magic to reveal itself.

The architect Philip Johnson came to my studio straight from the Four Seasons restaurant, which was located in the Seagram Building that Philip designed. As he was still in his overcoat and gloves, I had him walk onto the set and wave like he was hailing a taxi.

As he crossed the room, he noticed a table with snacks. Watching Philip go from the ultimate New York power-lunch spot straight to the Girl Scout Cookies in my studio was hysterical. We had to wipe the Do-si-dos crumbs off of his coat for the next shot.

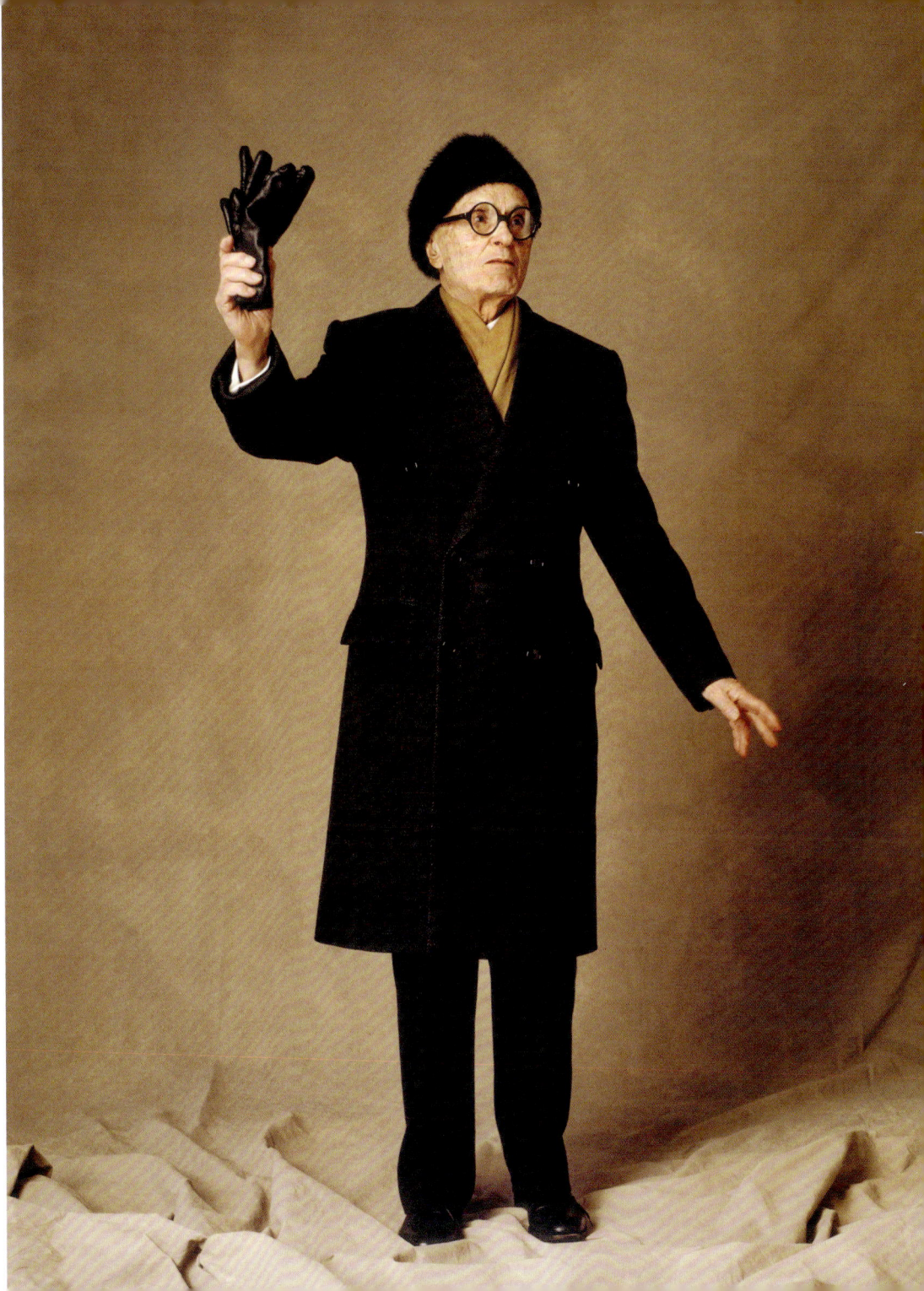

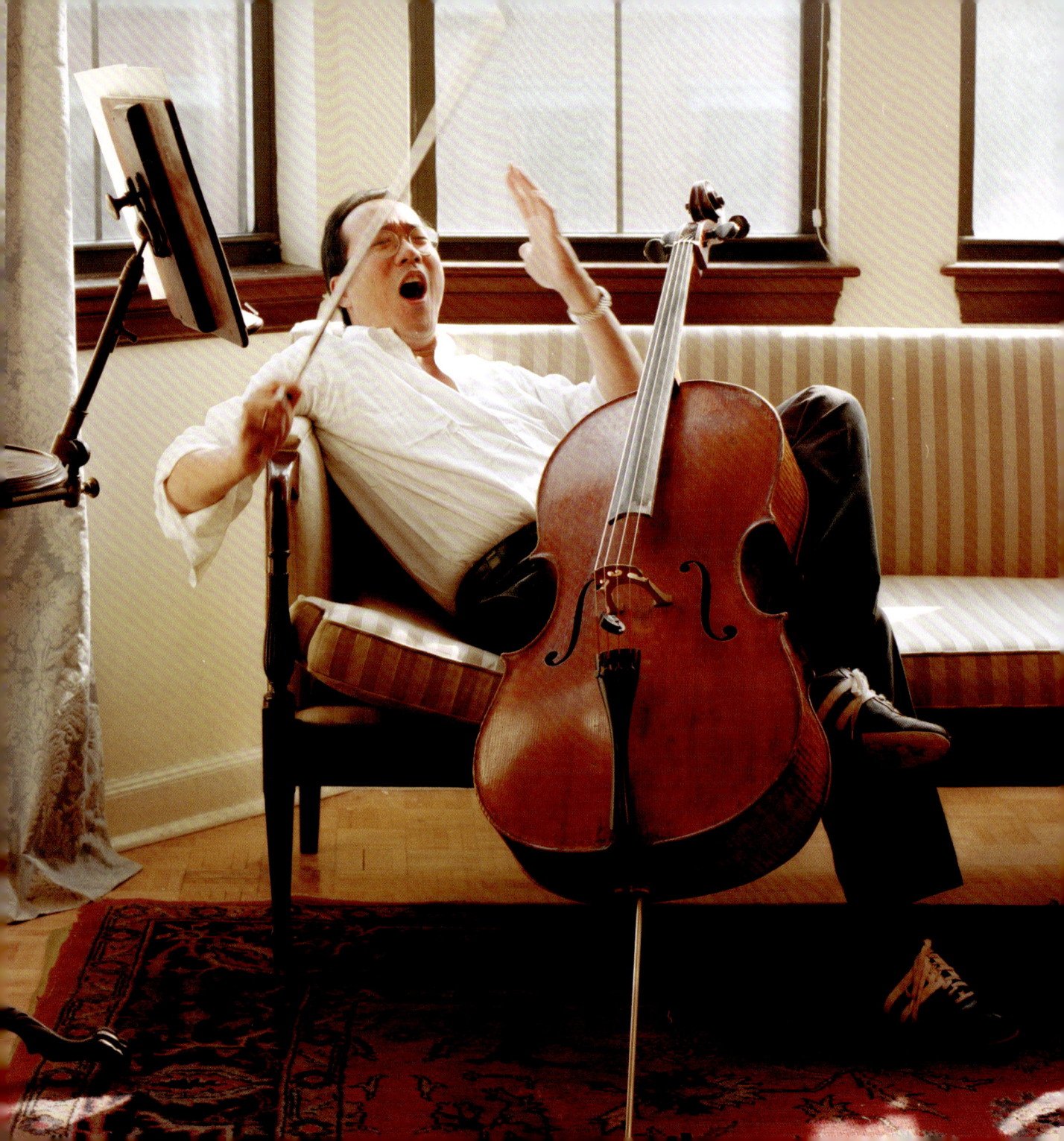

Yo-Yo Ma is one of the most joyful people I have ever met. At his local cello-repair shop in Boston, we took photos of him balanced on a sofa laughing and then from above, with his head on a workbench. It was a fun playdate.

Years later, we met after he had presented at a conference in New York. During his talk, he had said, "No matter what we do or how we do it, we are all on a search for human connection." His cello is his instrument to connect with others. I feel the same exact way about my camera.

After the conference, our time together was rushed and the shoot wasn't working. As the minutes ticked away, I panicked and yelled,

"CONNECT WITH ME!"

Like letting the clutch out on a hill and giving it gas, he was suddenly right there with me.

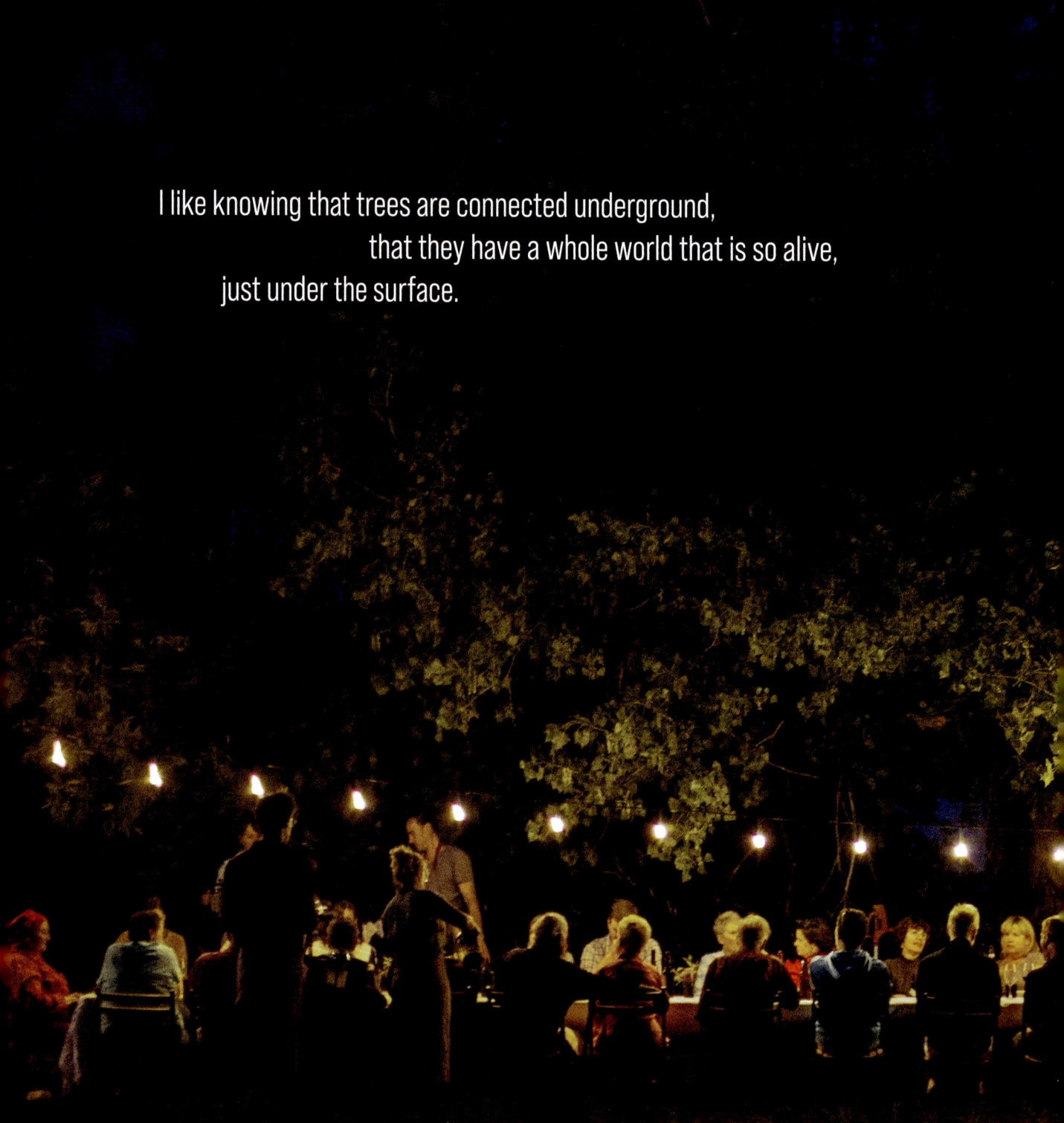

I like knowing that trees are connected underground,
that they have a whole world that is so alive,
just under the surface.

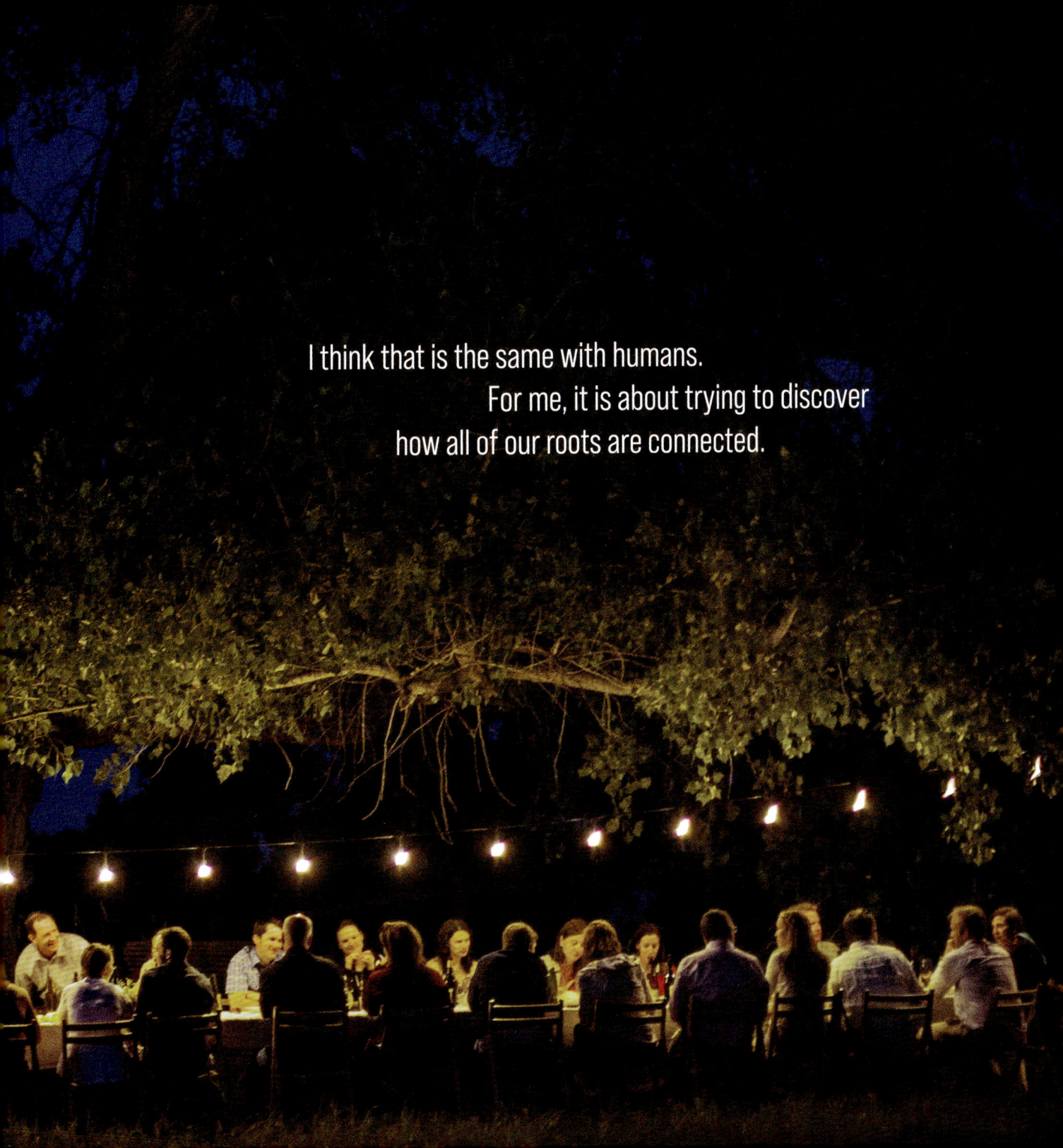

I think that is the same with humans.
For me, it is about trying to discover
how all of our roots are connected.

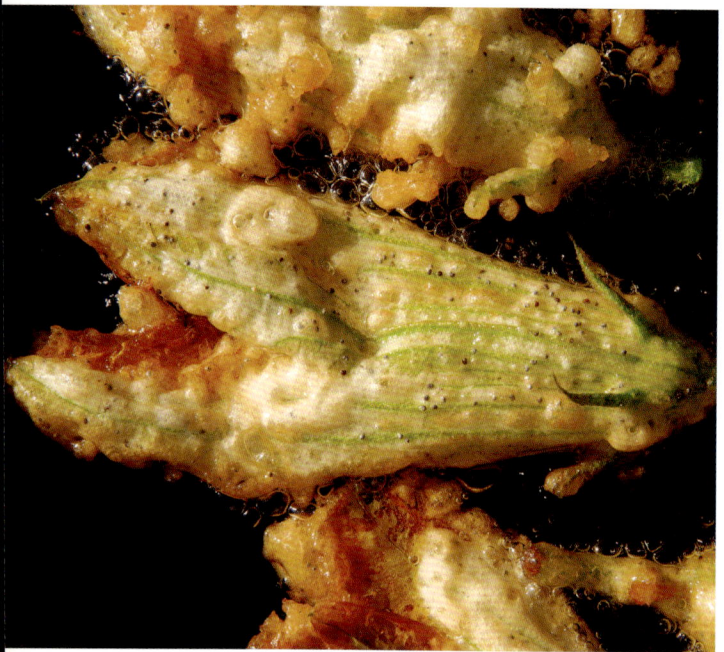

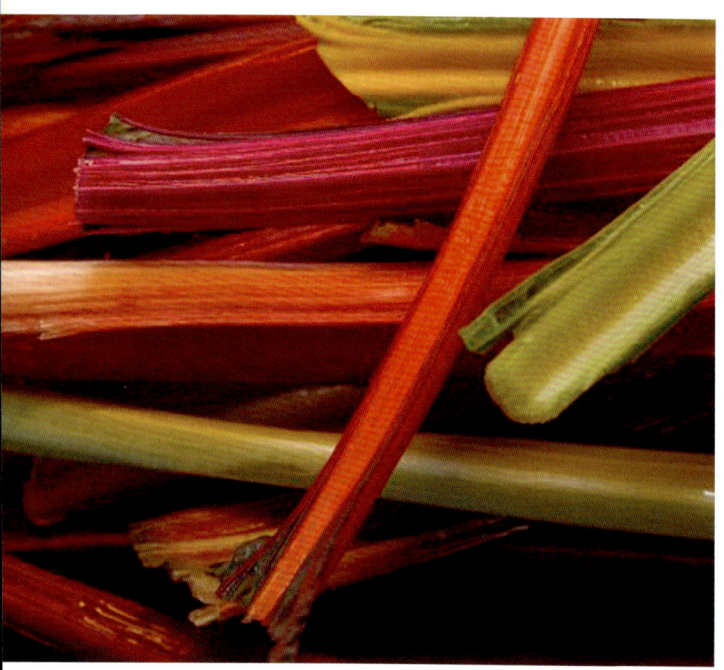

Meadow Lark Farm Dinners drives their converted bus to different local farms in Boulder, Colorado. There, they set up at the edge of the field to cook one sitting each night for forty-four people. Their long dining table is placed near the field where most of the produce they cooked was harvested. I was invited there to take pictures. Taking a deep dive with all of my senses, I often wandered through the fields alone and sometimes even lay down for a quick nap. I took photos of the fresh compost, the used pink borscht spoons, and the shadows—I love shadows! I held my camera just above the hot oil of sizzling, fresh squash blossoms. I got my lens steamed up over boiling pots of fresh peas. I pointed my camera everywhere except where it would normally have gone and found beauty and joy under the stars.

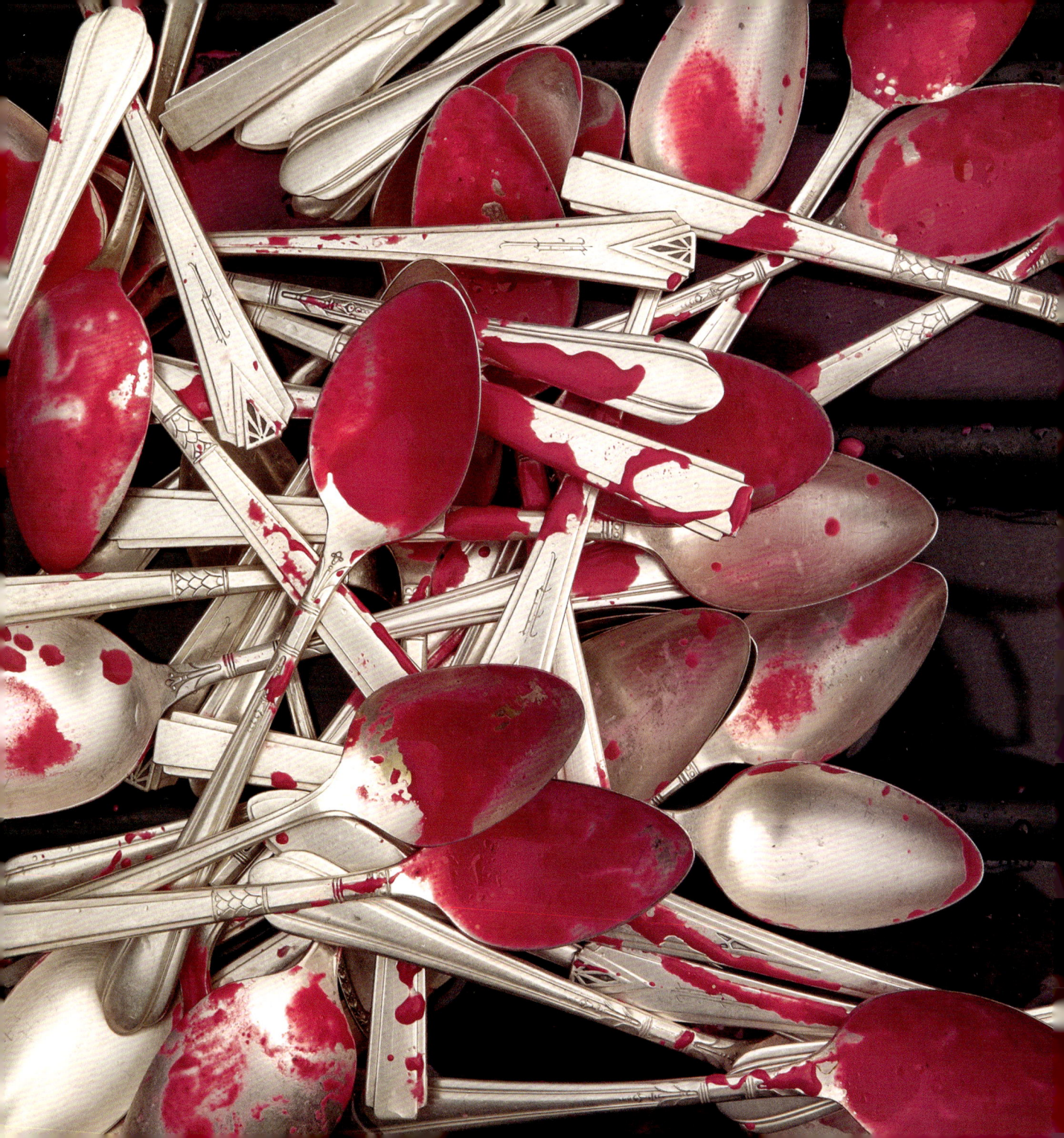

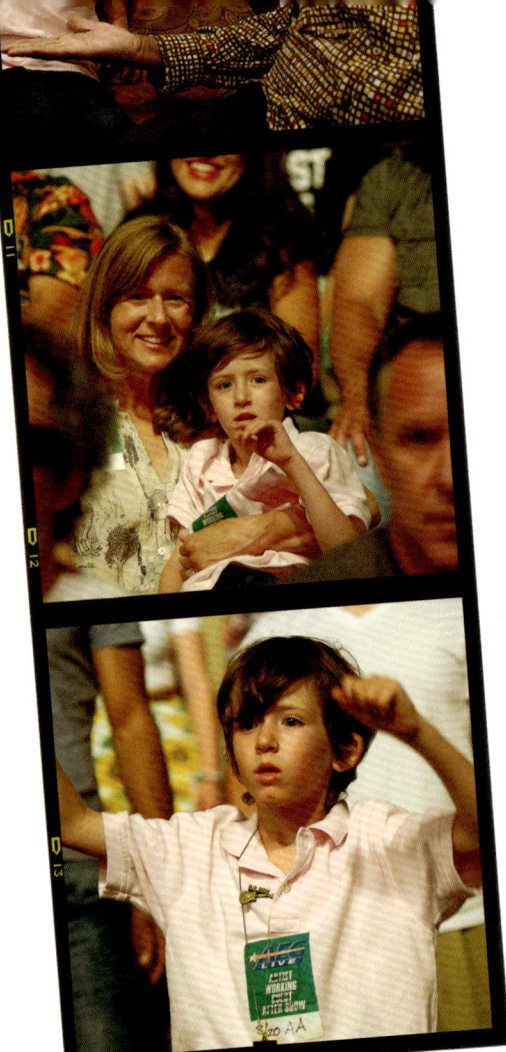

When Jackson was six, he was really into knock-knock jokes. He'd tell them wherever he went to whomever he met—including B.B. King, whom I had recently photographed. We took Jackson on B.B.'s tour bus before a performance at Red Rocks to say hello, and he immediately started telling the famous blues man joke after joke. B.B. loved every punch line. After five minutes I said, "We should probably go now . . ."

B.B. asked, "Why? Where are you going?"

So Jackson told him the rest of the jokes he knew.

Finally, we left the bus and went to the show. It was packed. In the middle of his set, B.B. saw Jackson in the audience and yelled out, "There is Jackson! Hey, Jackson!" He reached into his pocket, pulled out a pendant, and threw it to my son. It was like that Coke ad from the 1970s, with Mean Joe Greene throwing the kid his jersey. It felt like it was all in slow motion as the crowd watched the pendant arc through the air.

WHEN JACKSON CAUGHT IT. THE WHOLE AUDIENCE EXPLODED INTO APPLAUSE.

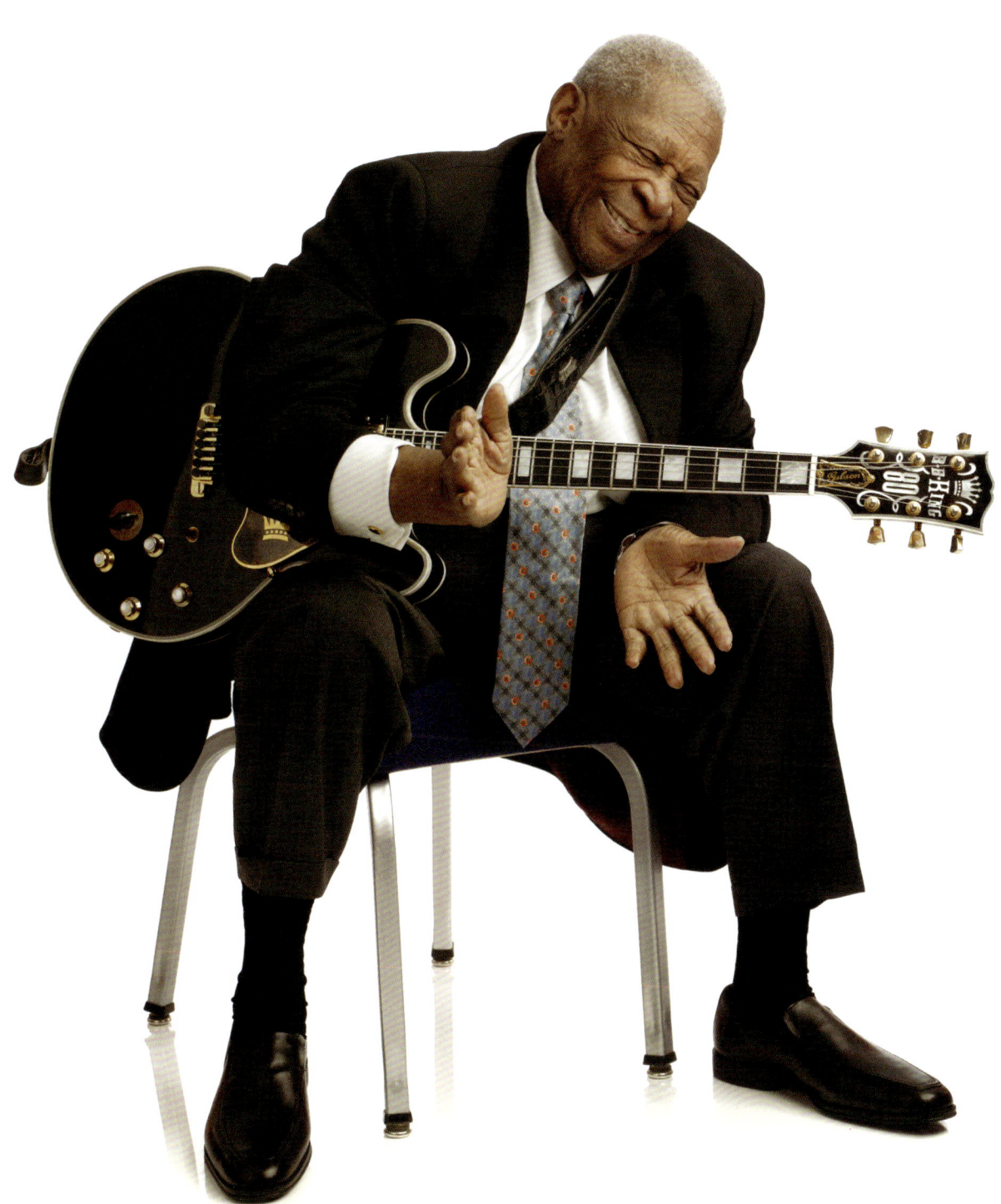

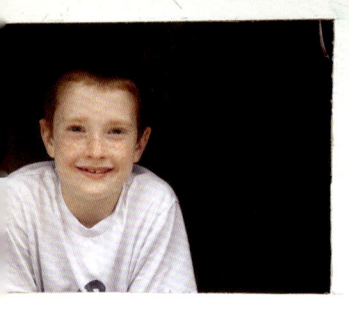
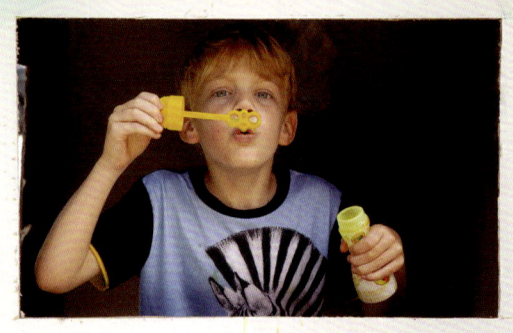
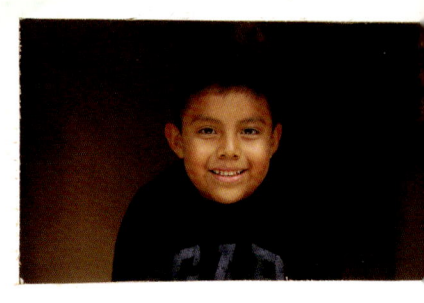

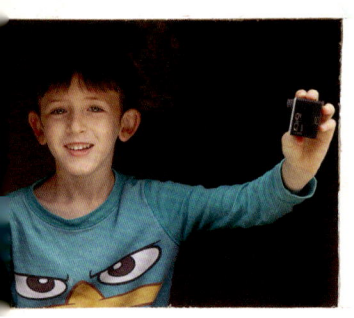

On the last day before elementary school let out for summer, my wife, Stephie, took a big corrugated box, painted it white, and cut a square in it to use as our set for a photo shoot. The kids climbed inside and stuck their heads out of the opening.

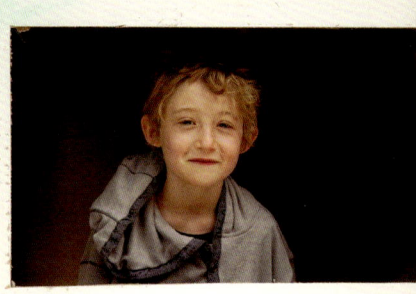

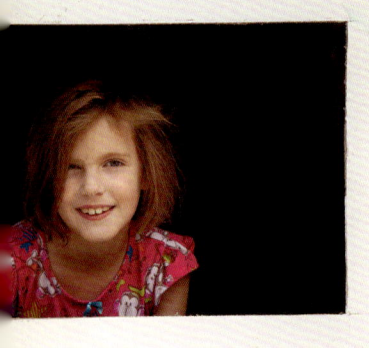
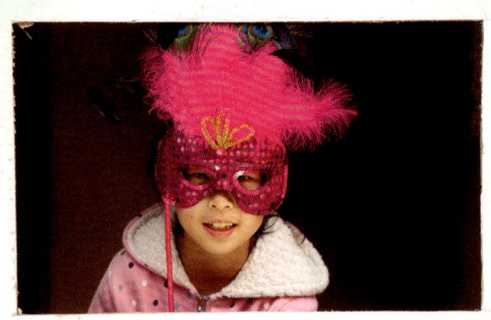
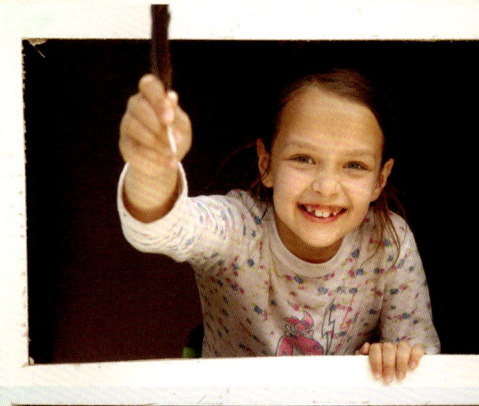

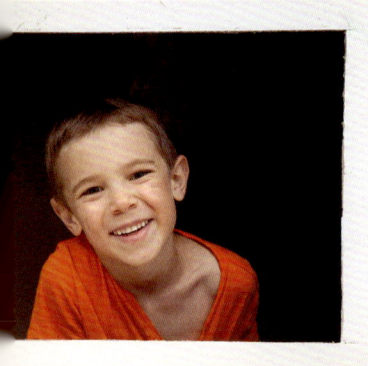
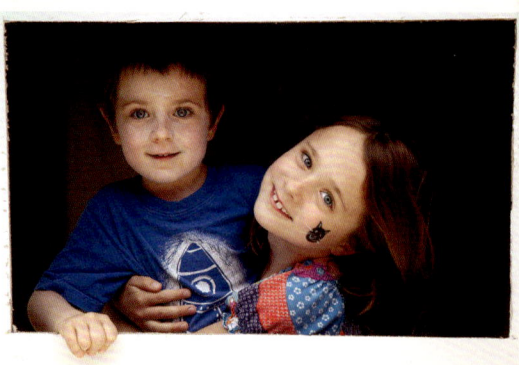
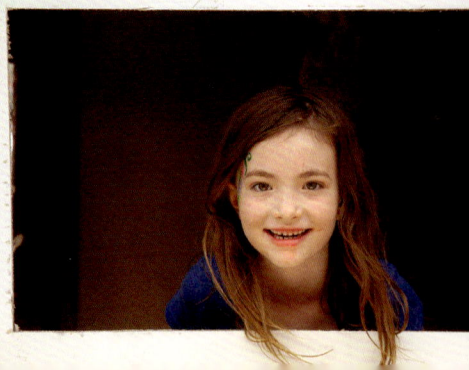

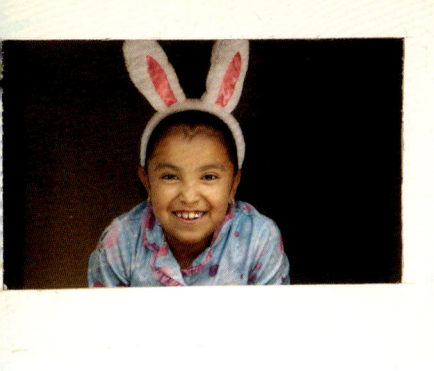
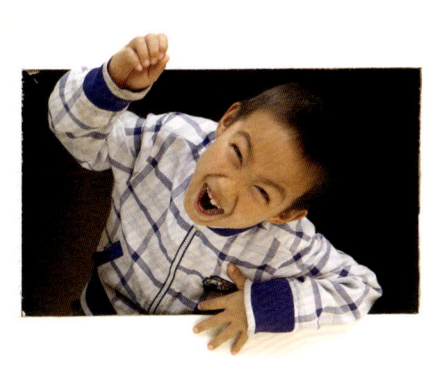
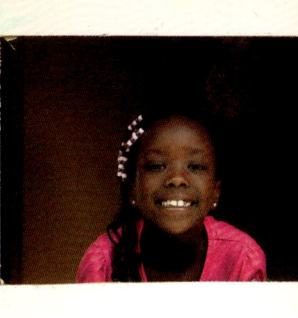
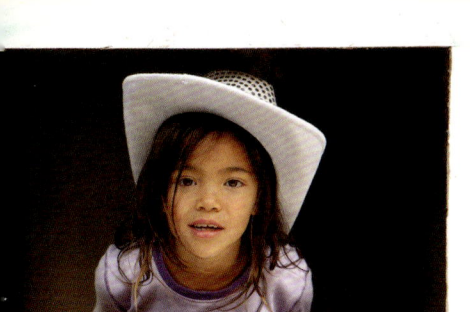
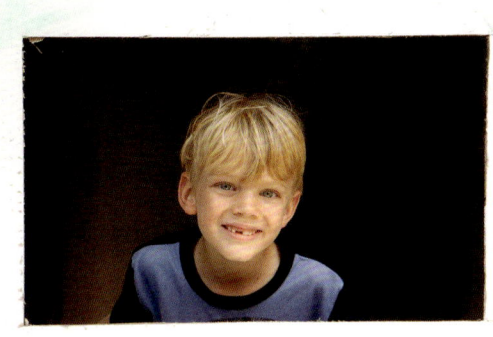
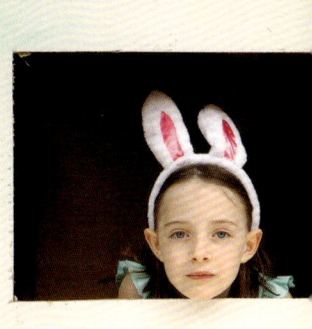
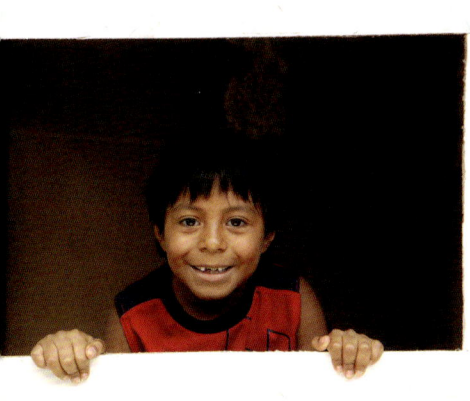

The genius of this idea is that the moment the kids got in the box, they were at ease and felt totally comfortable having their picture taken. It was like they were in control in that tiny space, which is exactly what most first graders need to feel.

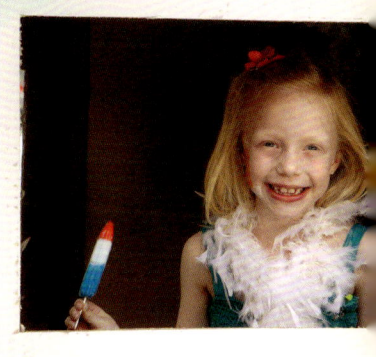
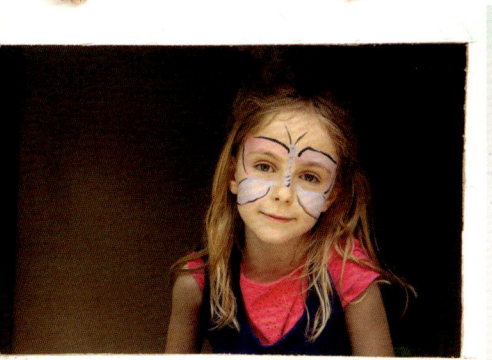
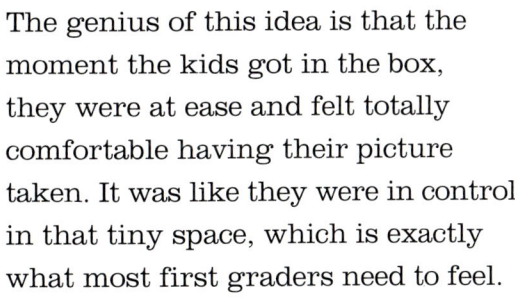
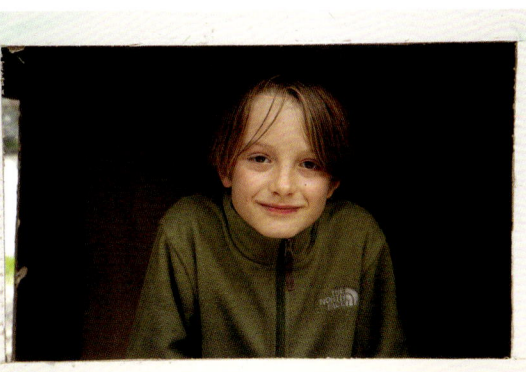
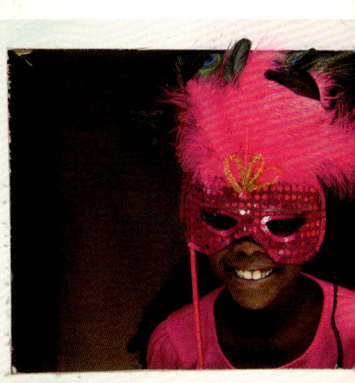

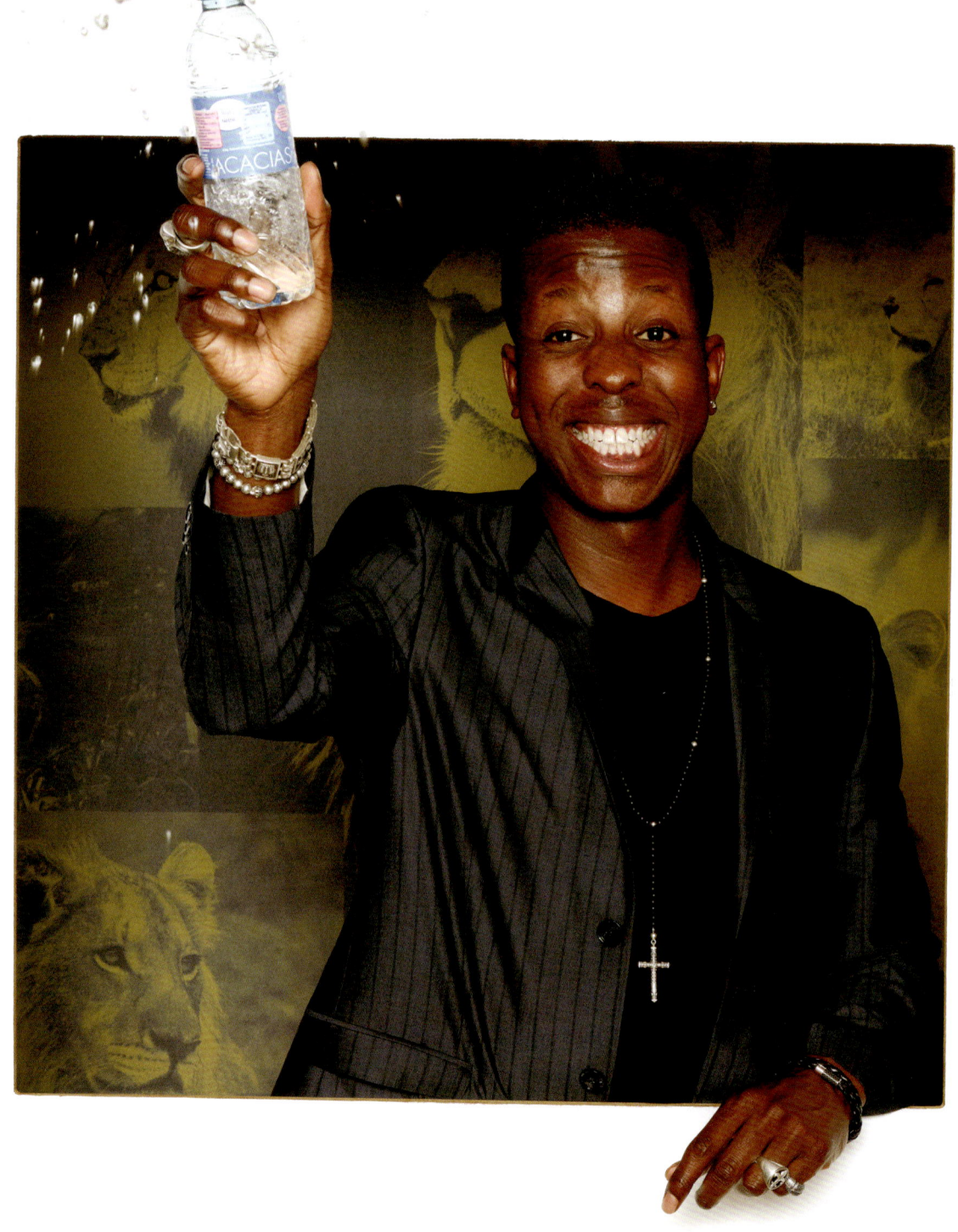

That summer, I did a photo shoot for Instagram on the beach in Cannes. It was backstage at the event where the world's top advertising people gathered each year.

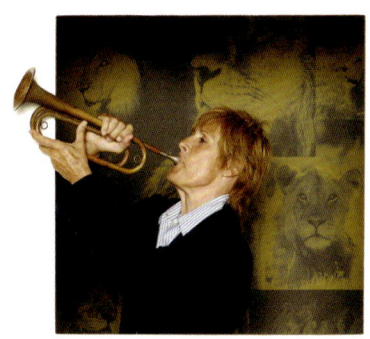

We had a wooden box built, modeled on the cardboard one Stephie had created weeks before. It was sturdier, a bit more elegant, but basically the same big box with a cutout square where people could be photographed.

What I love about this series of pictures is how each one is so different. Mark Ronson. Julia Louis-Dreyfus. Jamie Oliver. Diana Nyad. Lots of advertising creatives and execs. They all made this little square their own, like Jamal Edwards when he threw his water at me. In the few minutes I had, I would beg, cajole, light little fires, and play with bigger fires. Champagne was launched and trumpets blared. It was all great fun, quick interactions so fast you had no time to get your guard up. By the time you actually could start thinking, the shoot was over.

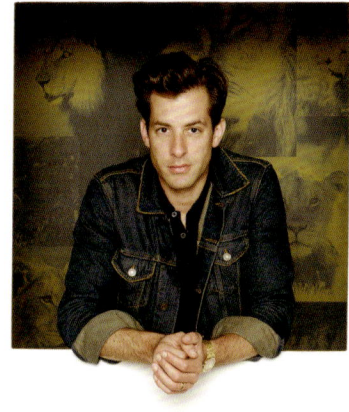

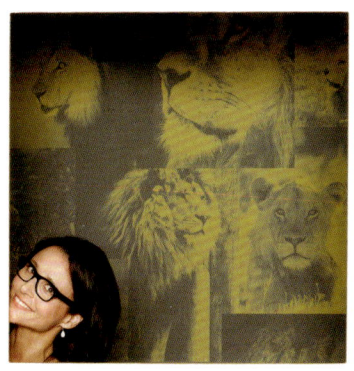

One spring evening, Stephie and I closed the Pittsburgh studio and walked down Penn Avenue to see all the other galleries open for the Friday night art walk called Unblurred. We were alone and had the whole evening to roam—a rare luxury! Outside of Kraynick's Bike Shop, Celeste Jones had set up a table of T-shirts promoting her passion, "A Life of Cycles," which wasn't about bikes at all but finding joy in all the cycles of life. Celeste told me she teaches happiness workshops. When I asked what the workshops are like, she burst out in a gorgeous, boisterous laugh. Suddenly, we were all laughing with her, proving the power of infectious joy.

... WASN'T ABOUT BIKES AT ALL BUT FINDING JOY IN ALL THE CYCLES OF LIFE.

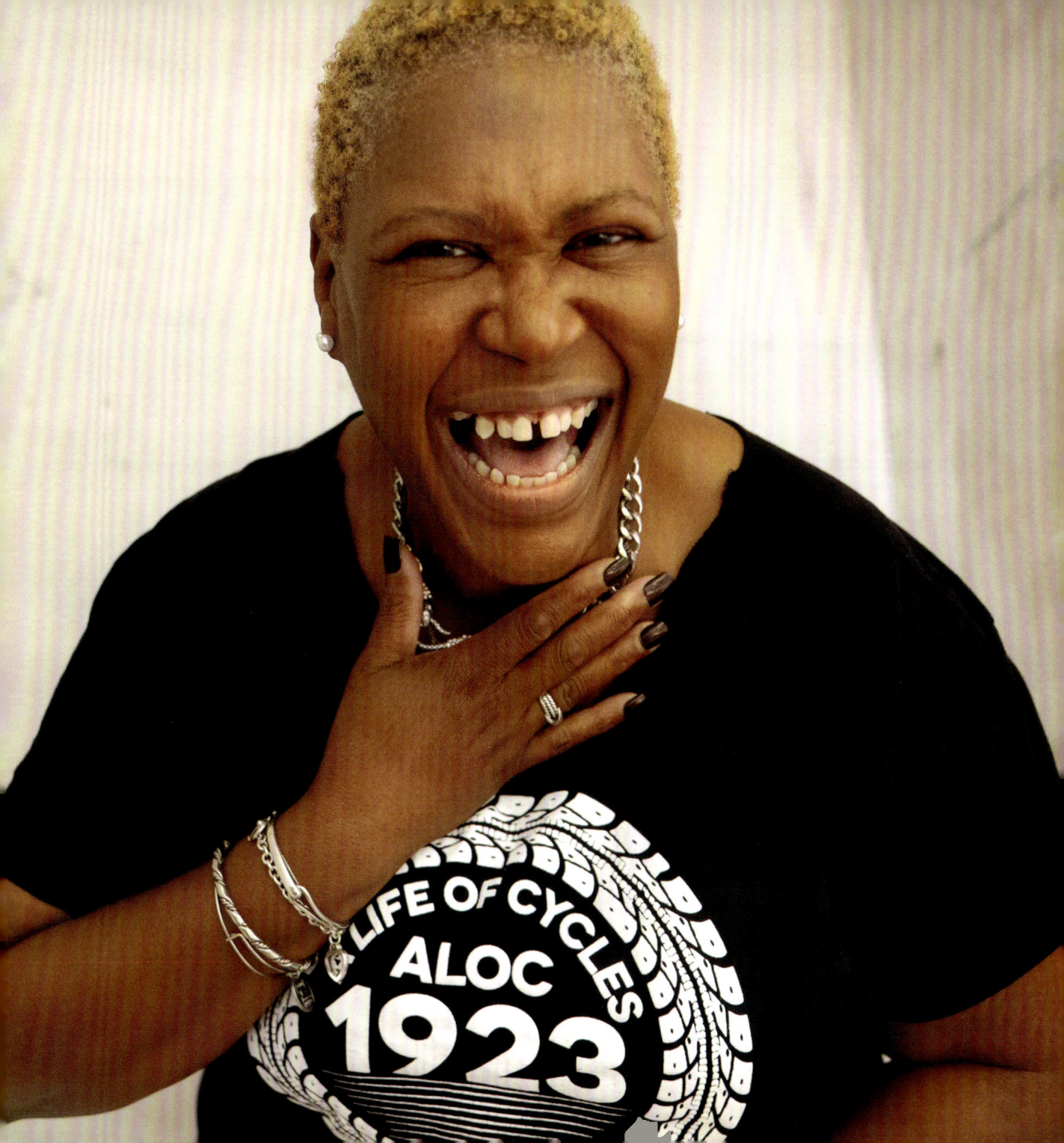

I don't always know where the pictures are going when I pick up the camera. I'm hired now for my experience, which allows me to take risks and create on the spot.

I went to Alabama, where Ewan McGregor was filming *Big Fish*, to do a shoot about his love of smoking—an idea that seems so last century. (I have never smoked, but cigarette smoke is one of the best props ever.) I saw this huge taxidermy lion tucked into a prop room in the old school where they were filming. I set up a light and stuck my head in the lion's mouth, just to make sure it was safe in there. Ewan McGregor came in, lit up, and took his chance.

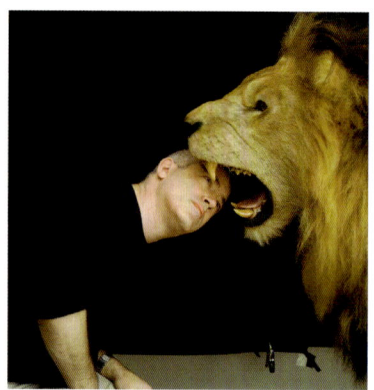

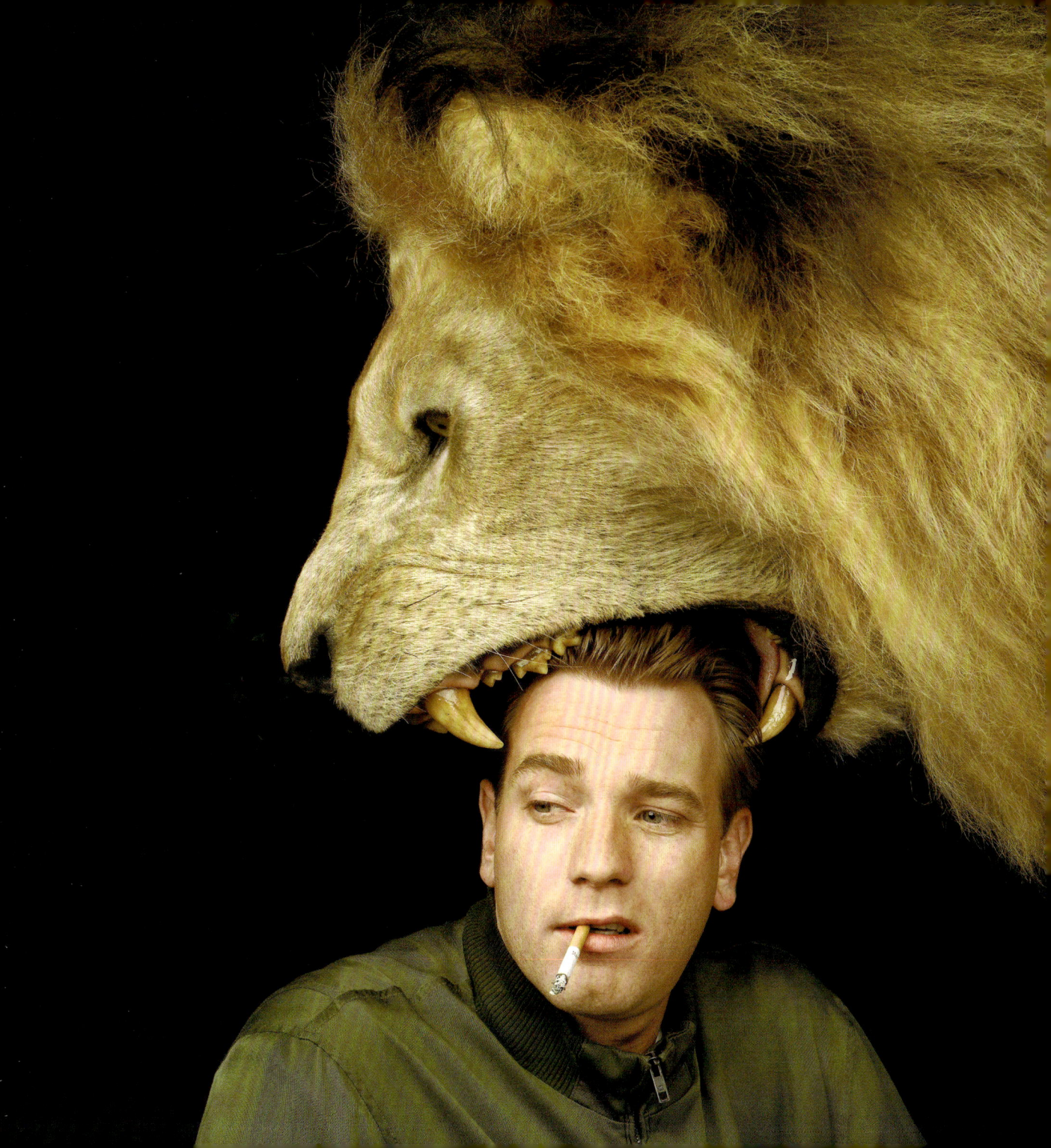

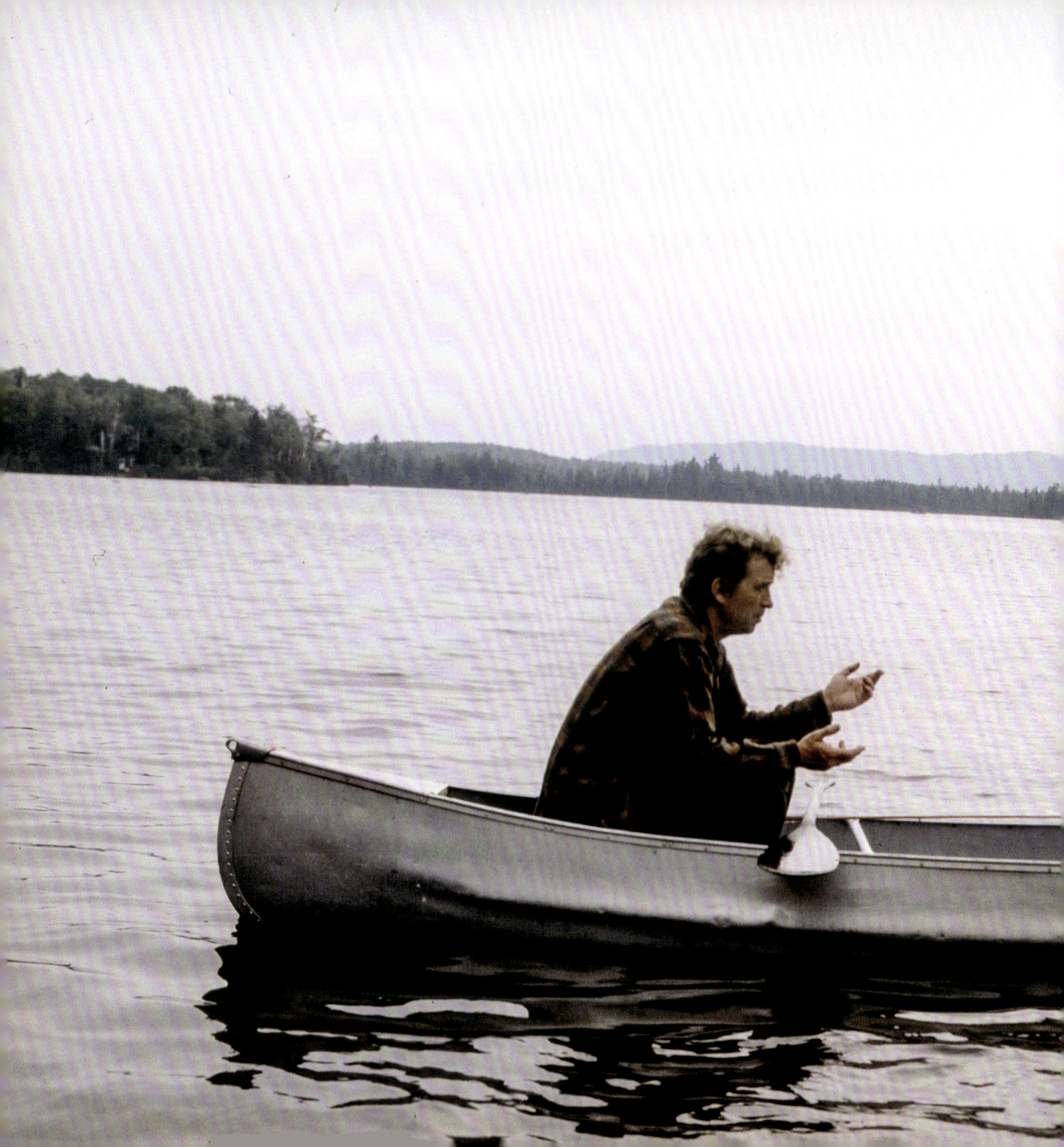

When I took this photo of William Wegman and one of his weimaraners, it struck me as the perfect portrait of a couple out for a boat ride at sunset.

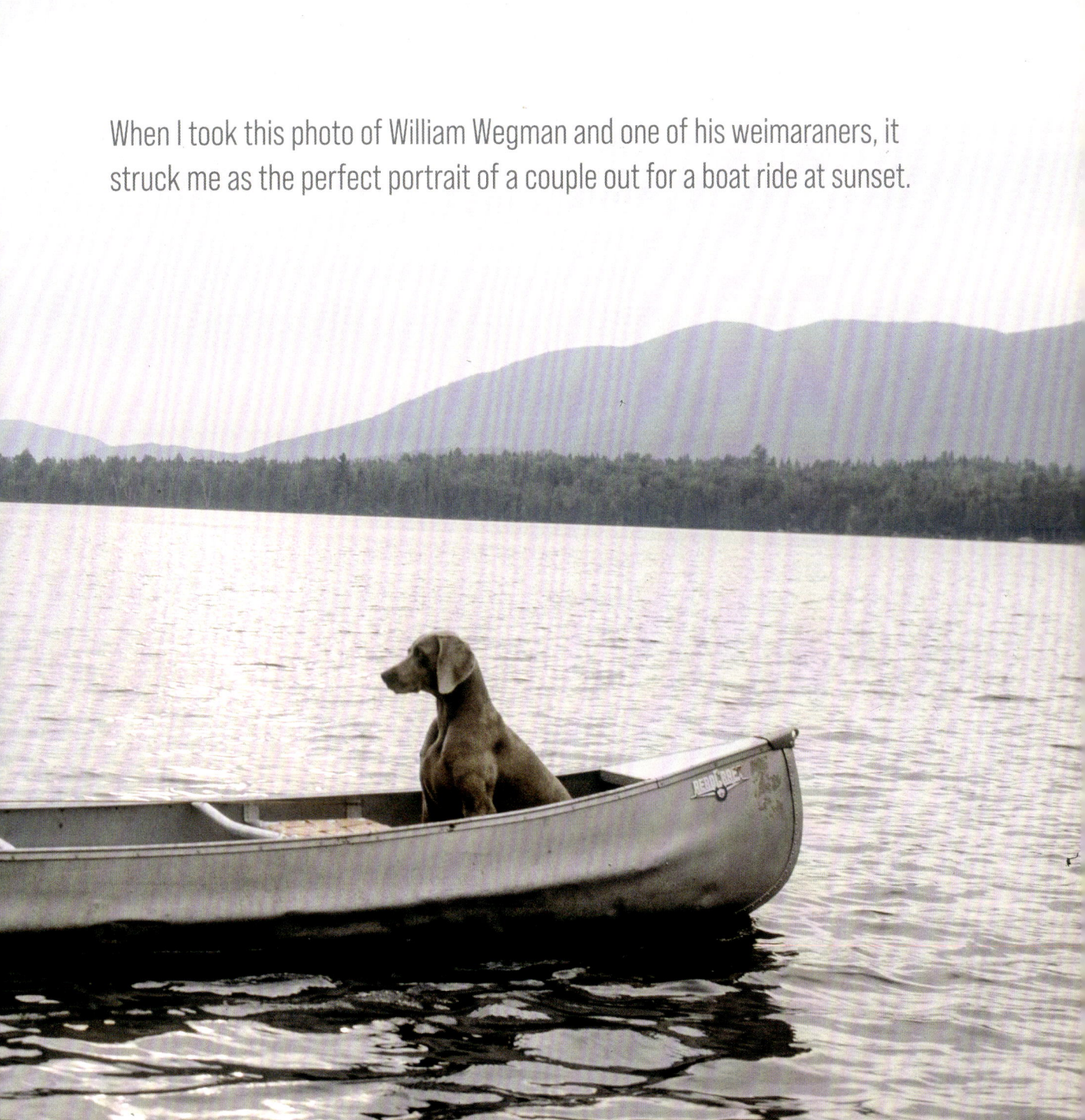

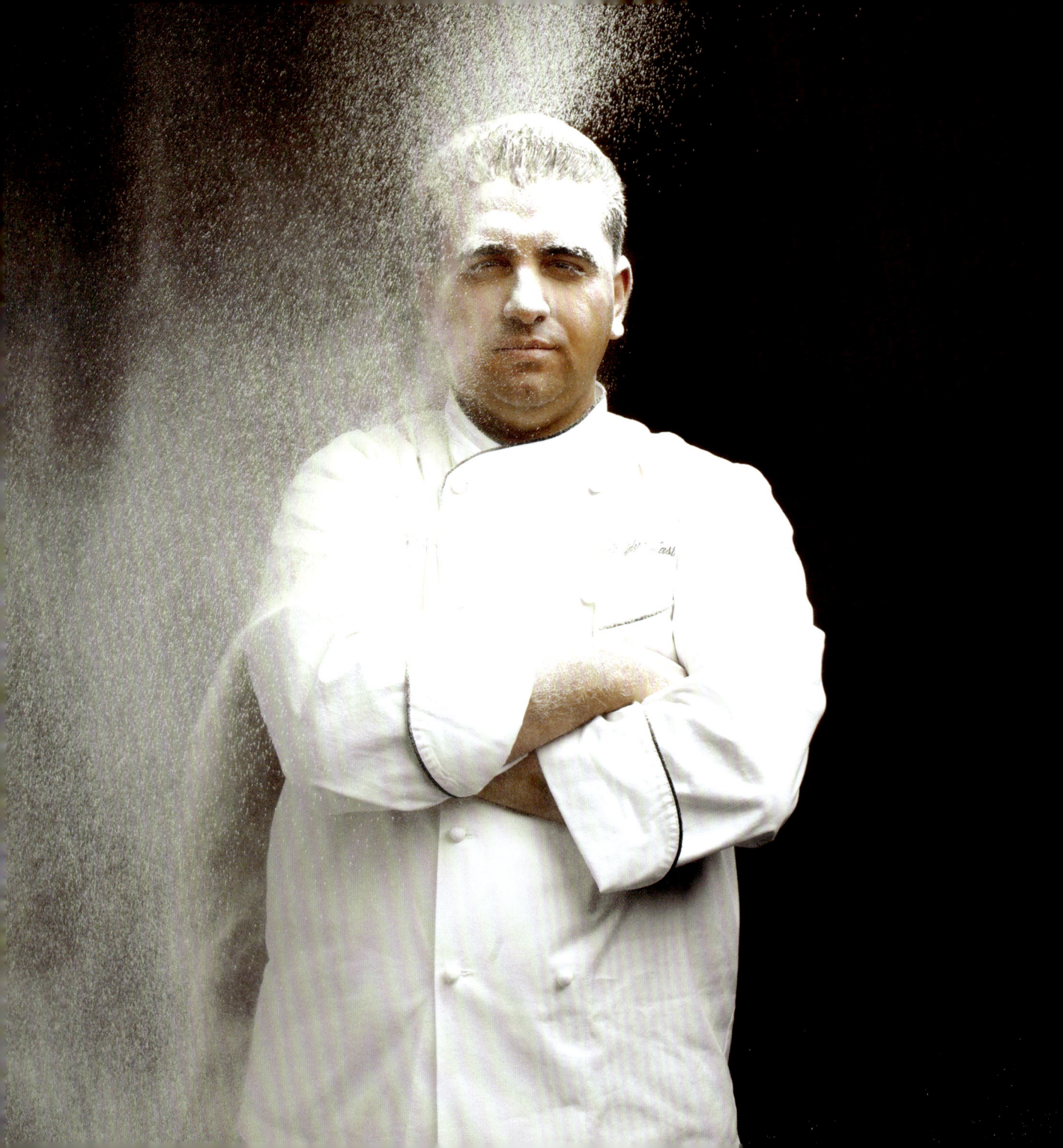

The *Cake Boss* shoot was a watershed moment. I was behind the camera with my face pressed against the viewfinder. I was photographing Buddy "Cake Boss" Valastro, Jr., in front of a backdrop Stephie had created, painted the color of chocolate. We were in the alley behind Buddy's bakery in Hoboken, New Jersey, and an assistant was balanced on a ladder with a huge sifter full of flour. All the clients and production people were looking on. I directed Buddy to stand there with his arms folded, staring at the camera.

For a second, I paused. For the first time in my life, I felt like I owned the moment. I knew how I got there. I knew what I was doing. I knew where it was going. I had always taken responsibility for my work, but something clicked and I finally appreciated my hands on the wheel driving the shoot.

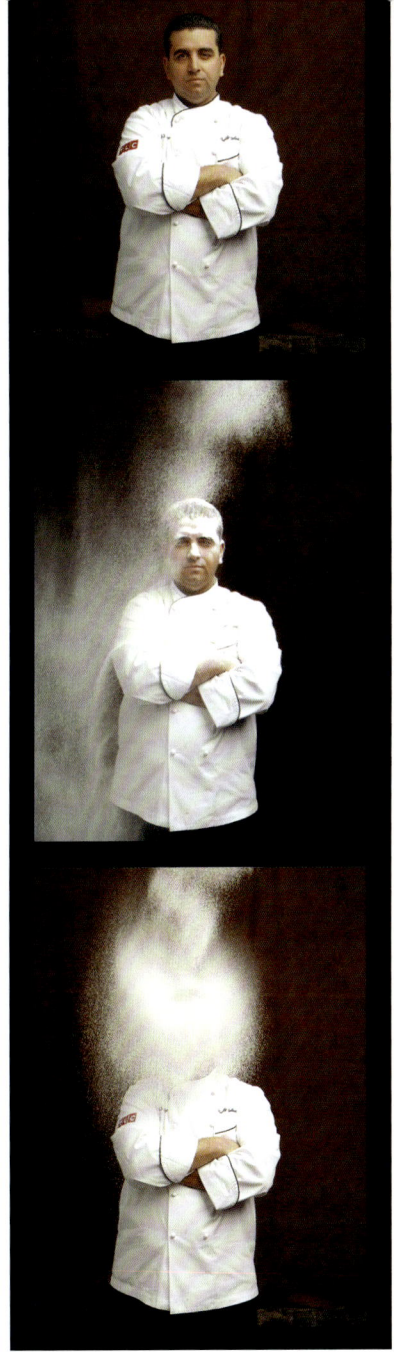

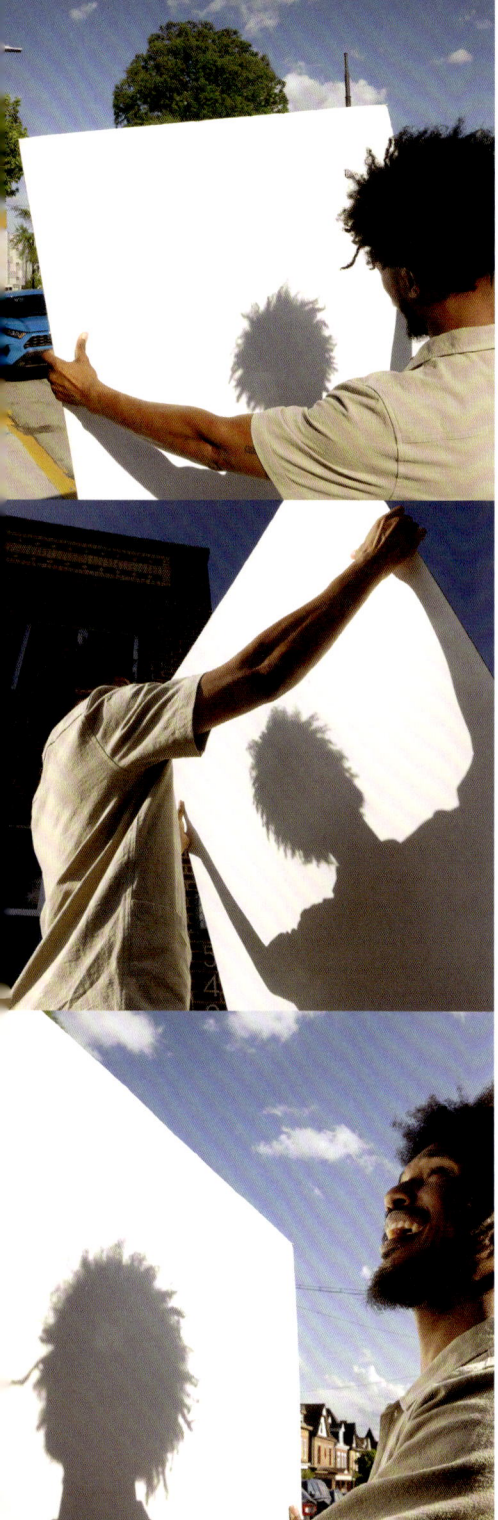

A local Pittsburgh rapper named Mars Jackson came to my studio last spring. We had been trying to hook up for over a year, and finally we had a beautiful afternoon to take photos. As Mars walked up the street, he was backlit with hard afternoon sun, and all I could make out was his dramatic shadow. Mars told me that seeing his shadow in front of him reminded him of scenes from *Peter Pan*.

I grabbed a whiteboard, used it like a shadow mirror, and crawled on my back along the sidewalk, asking Mars to move in and out of focus. Then we played with the graffiti wall around the corner, the light reflecting off the beauty parlor across the street and the gardens of a local restaurant. Mars Jackson has a smile that is totally infectious.

THE BEAUTIFUL THING ABOUT MARS IS THAT HE BELIEVES HIS SMILE MAKES HIM WHO HE IS.

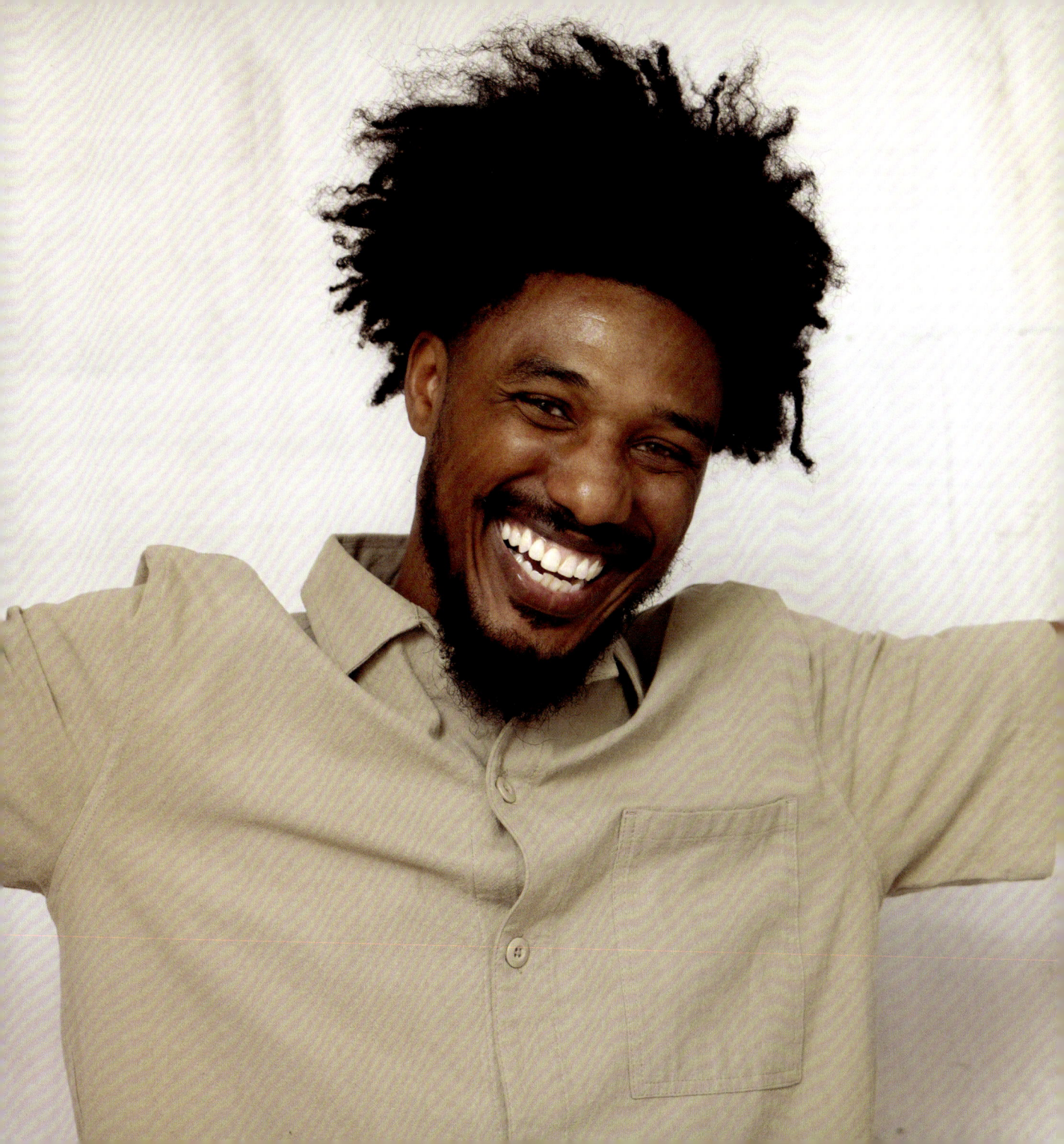

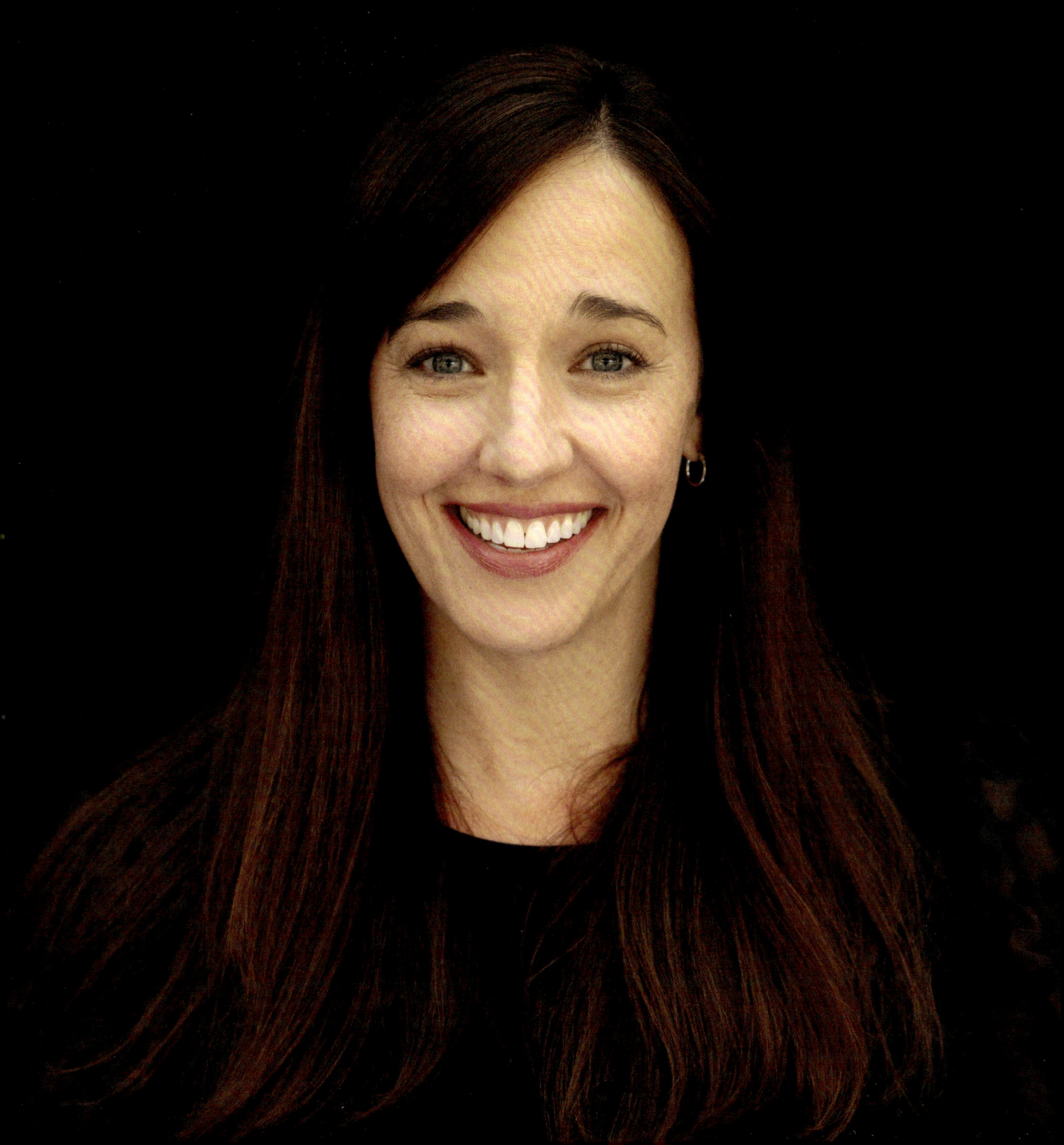

For decades, a group of corporate communications executives has gotten together every year at a retreat at Lake Minnesuing in Wisconsin. One year, I was invited to come speak and take photos. Improvising, I pulled a black tablecloth off one of the dining tables and taped it to a window outdoors on the patio.

I directed each person to stand in front of the rest of the group and pose. The next person had to push them out of the way and then make it about themselves. Shove, hip bump, twirl the person—it didn't matter. But it led to a wild exercise in total abandon and fun.

Later that night by the big fireplace, everyone gathered around to check out the pictures. I noticed one woman spent a long time looking at her photos, and she began to tear up. I asked what was wrong. "I'm not used to seeing myself in this way," she said. "I rarely allow myself to see my own beauty."

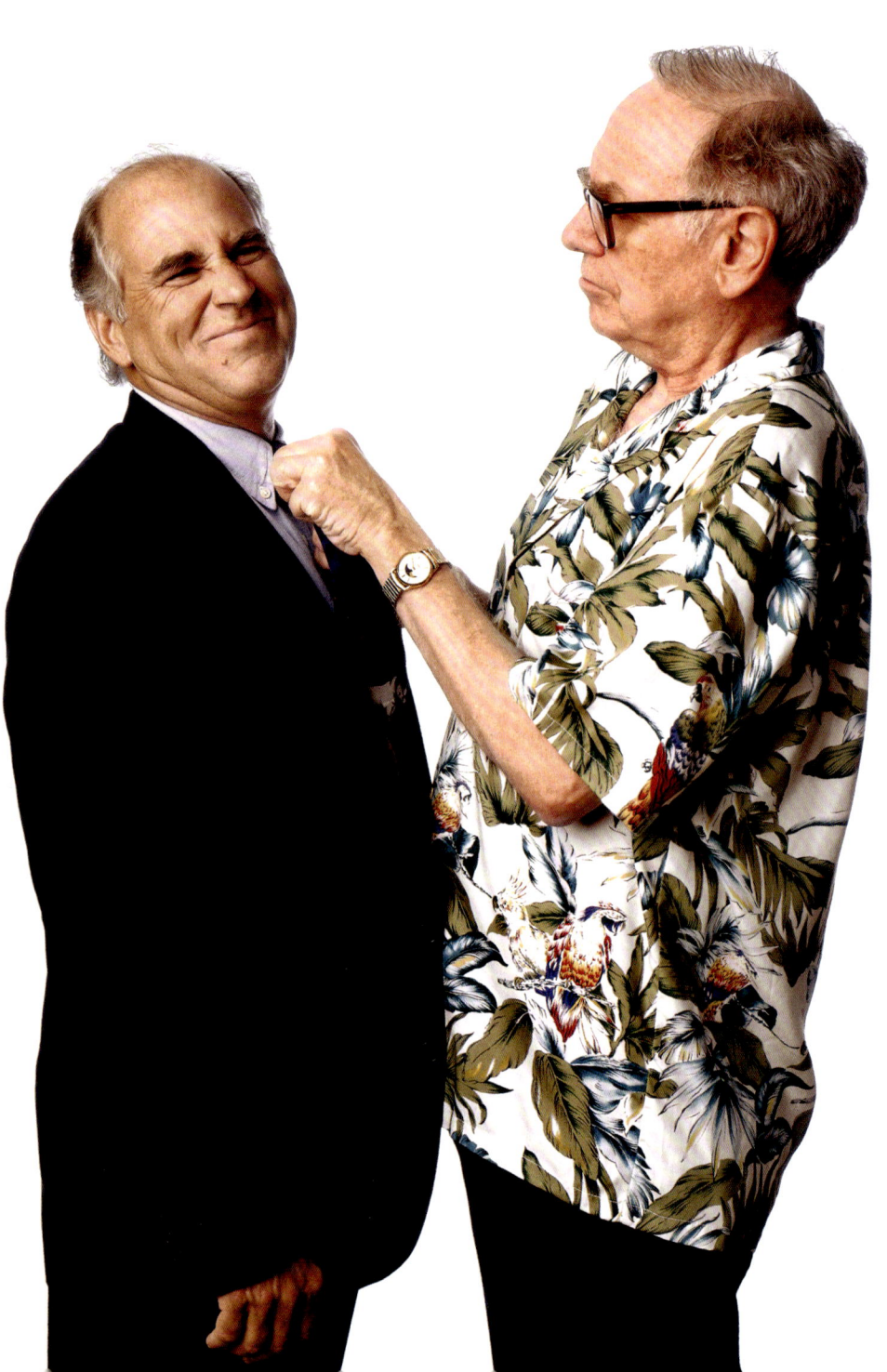

I am not sure if I should be proud of this, but my photo sessions are almost always fast. Executives who hate being photographed are not prepared for the shoots to be so painless. Celebrities who are on a tight schedule get to dinner early. I am like the pediatrician who is finished with the shot before the kid remembers to be afraid.

This photo is about a simple idea. I wanted to have these two Buffetts, Jimmy and Warren, dress up as each other. They were game. It all went really fast, but the kicker is the look Jimmy Buffett is giving the camera.

My friend Bob Feldman hung a huge print of this behind his desk at work. He says every morning when he walks in and sees Jimmy giving him that look, it launches his day on the right track.

Demeatria Boccella of FashionAFRICANA engaged me to photograph for *Childhood Lost*, a WQED Multimedia documentary about the adultification of young Black girls. It deals with the perception that Black girls are somehow more aggressive and less deserving of support and care.

For the ad shoot, I knew I had to allow the girls to open up in their own way and allow me to capture their age. They came to the set and shared with me what makes each one of them so extraordinary.

Some of the girls were really shy as they walked to a spot in front of my camera. Some danced onto the set, exuberantly swinging their long braids. My job was to allow them to be themselves.

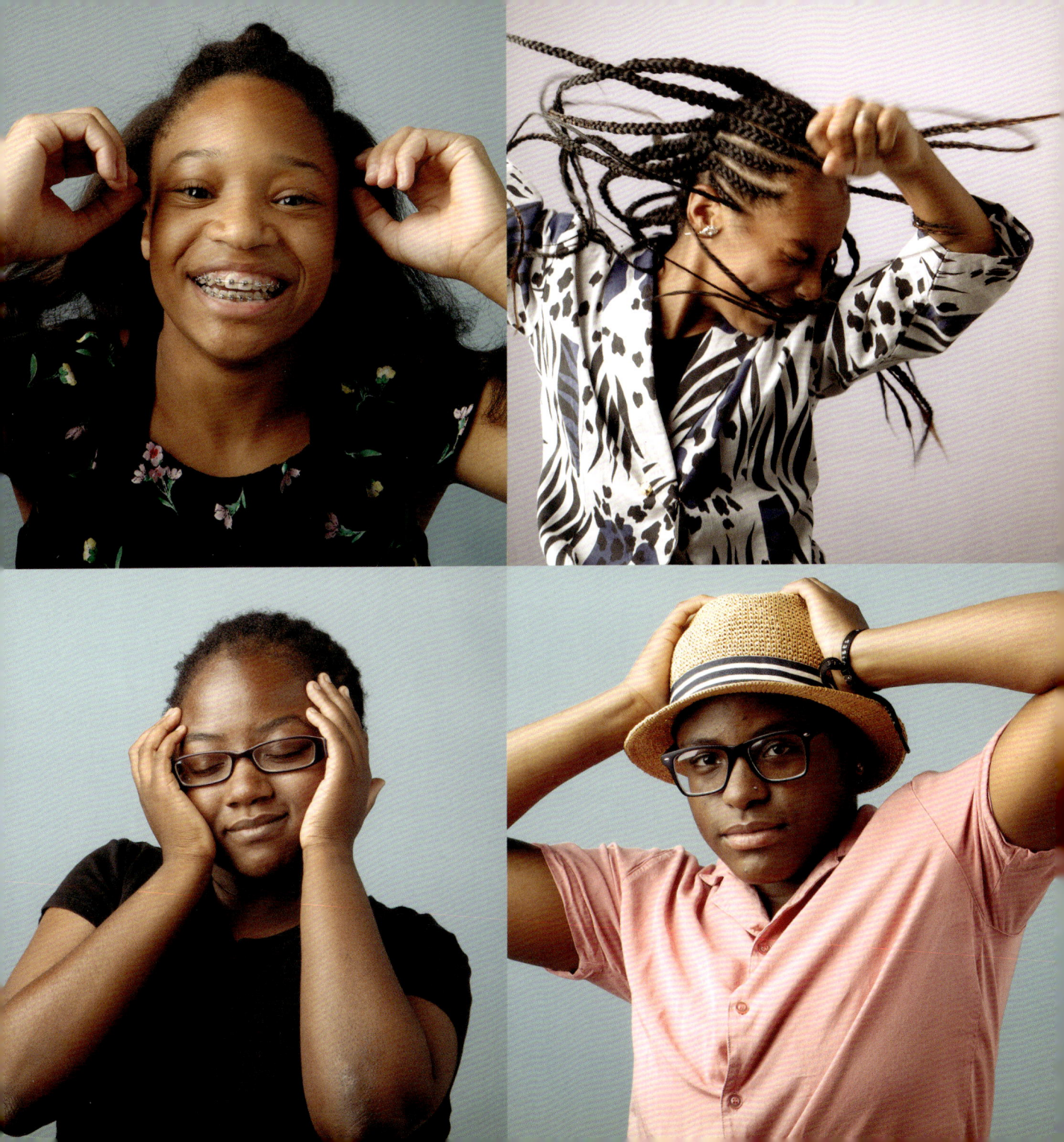

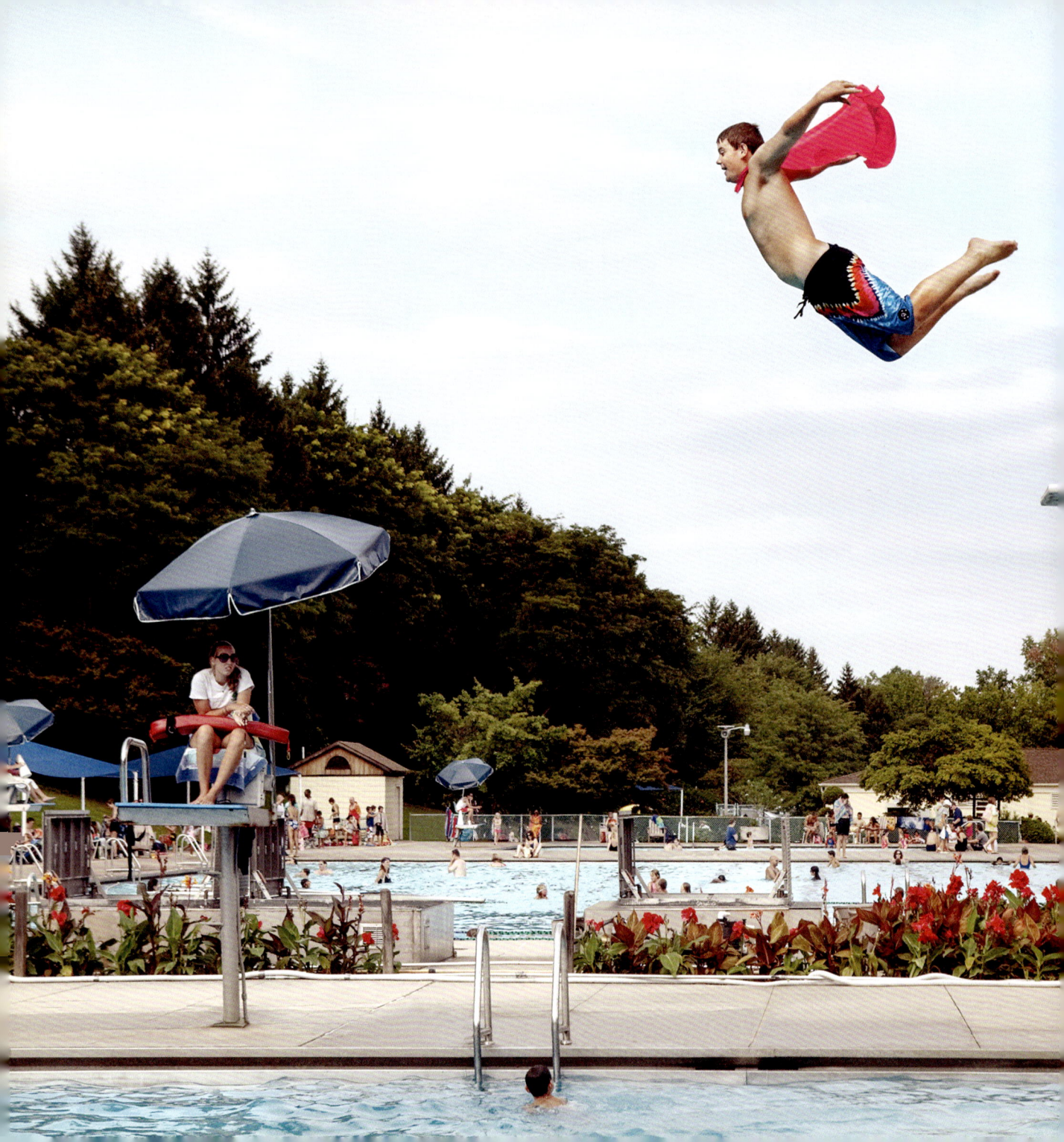

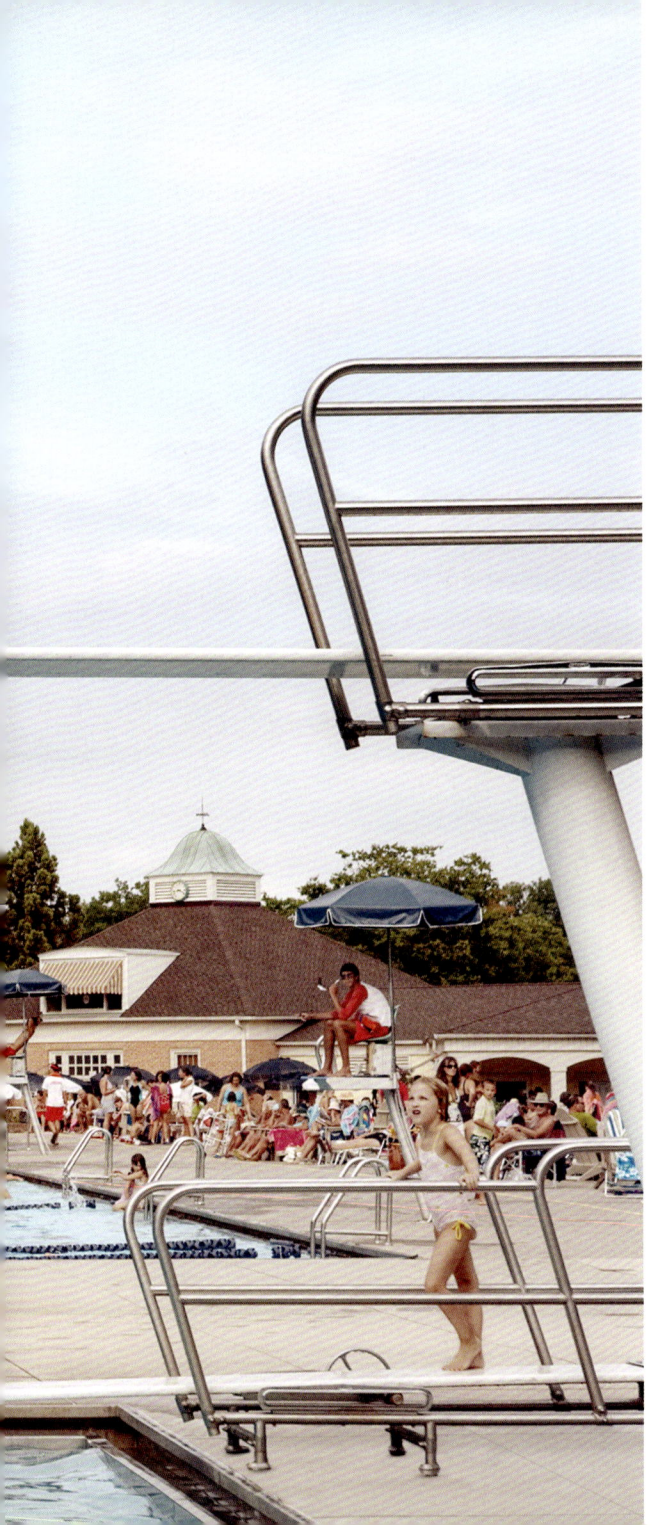

I always want to record things that thrill me, either with my camera or by taking mental pictures. But having a real-world record allows me to free space in my brain, kind of like erasing files to make room on my internal hard drive.

Every Labor Day in Maplewood, New Jersey, I would watch the kids drink in the last days of summer. Always with my camera in tow, I would lie for hours on my back under the high dive platforms taking pictures of kids falling through the sky.

THE KID WITH THE CAPE WAS A SURPRISE, A FLASHING SINGULAR MOMENT,

but he captured that feeling of freedom better than anyone.

I am often introduced as having photographed the Obamas. In a sea of photo shoots,

I doubt they would remember mine. Barack Obama had just won the Democratic

nomination for President, and as a lifetime liberal, I was beyond thrilled to meet

Michelle and Barack and shake their hands.

The shoot took place at a nursing home in Columbus, Ohio. A few minutes in, the

electricity went out. There was no time to panic; I kept taking pictures. Luckily, their

silhouettes were backlit by the window. They were cool in the dark. They were cool in

the light. I had Aretha turned up loud the whole time, and they were cool with that, too.

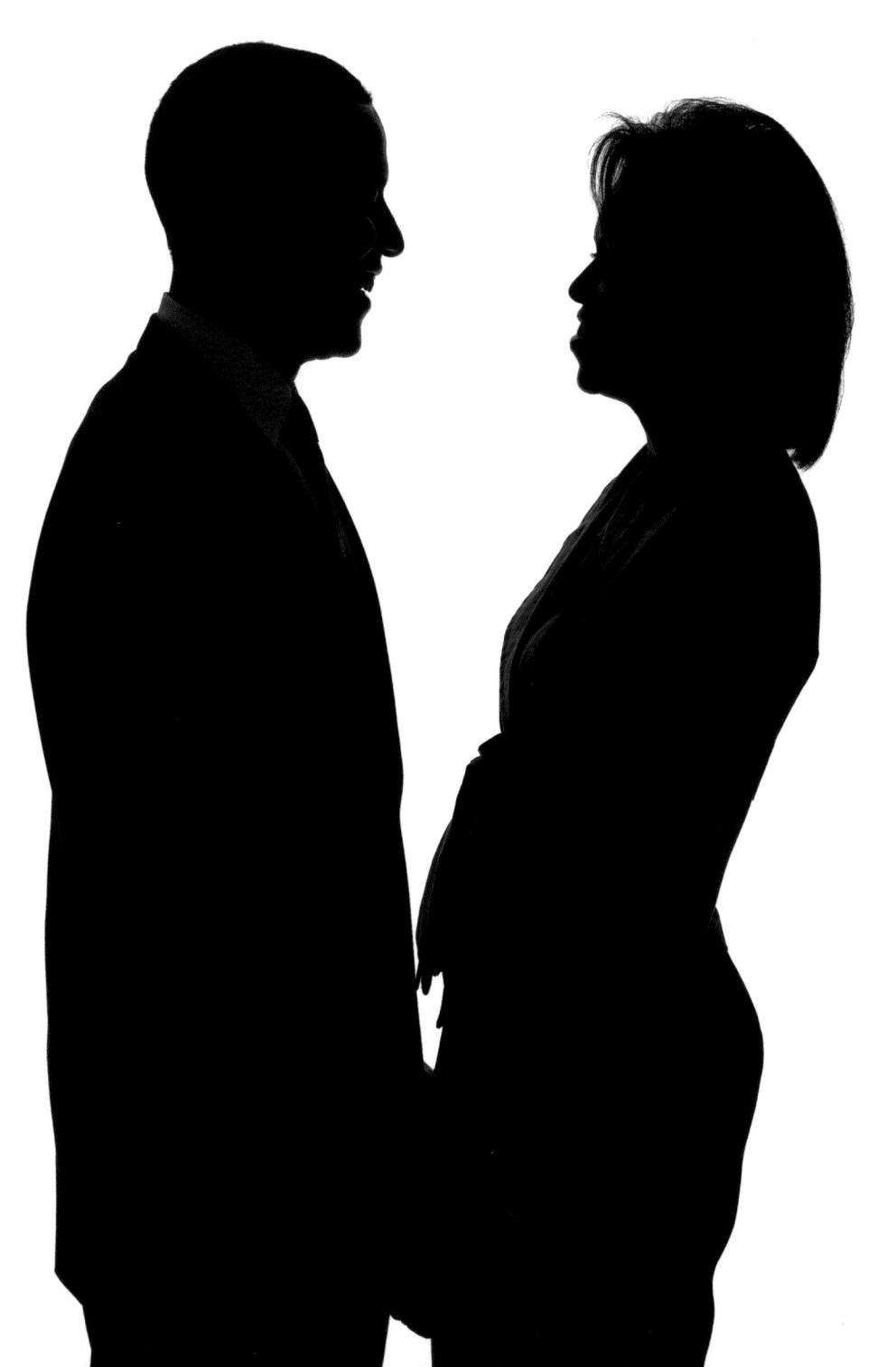

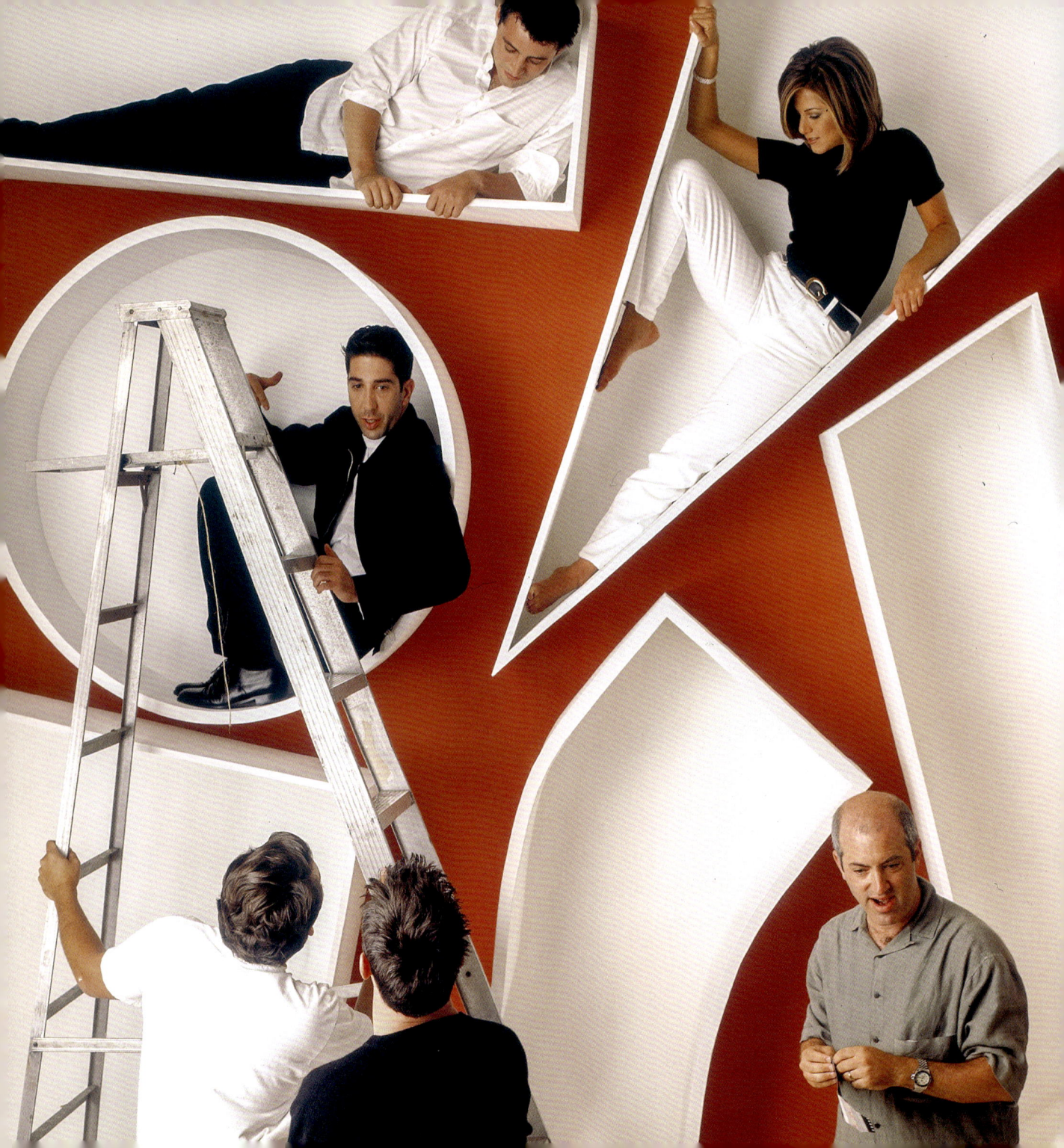

PHOTOS ARE THE ARTIFACTS OF OUR EXPERIENCE TOGETHER.

I STOLE THE IDEA FOR
THE SHOOT WITH JERRY
SEINFELD FROM ONE I
HAD DONE THE DAY
BEFORE WITH KERMIT
THE FROG. I LOVE
HOW JERRY MAKES
IT HIS OWN. IN SOME
OF THE SHOTS YOU
KNOW WHO HE IS,
BUT I REALLY LOVE
THE ONES WHERE
YOU NEED TO BE
IN ON THE JOKE,
LIKE THIS ONE.

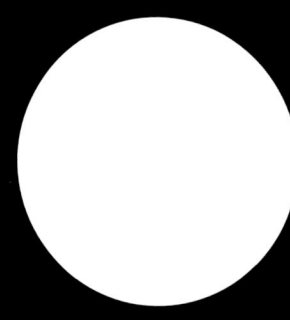

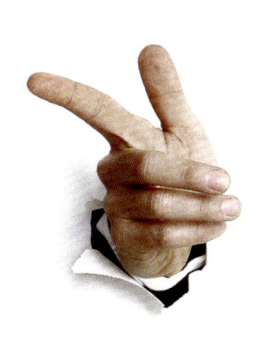
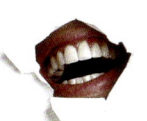
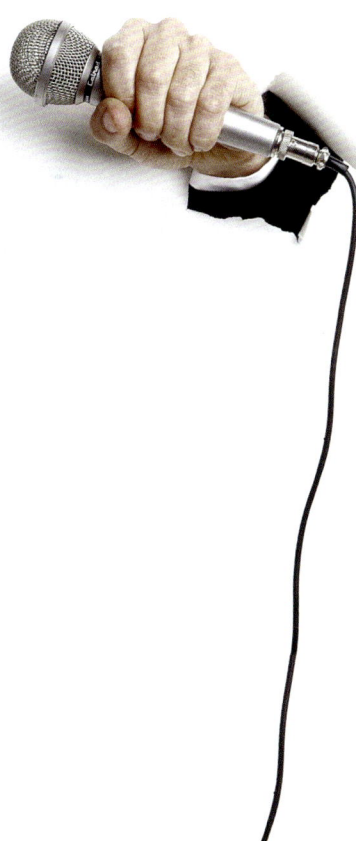

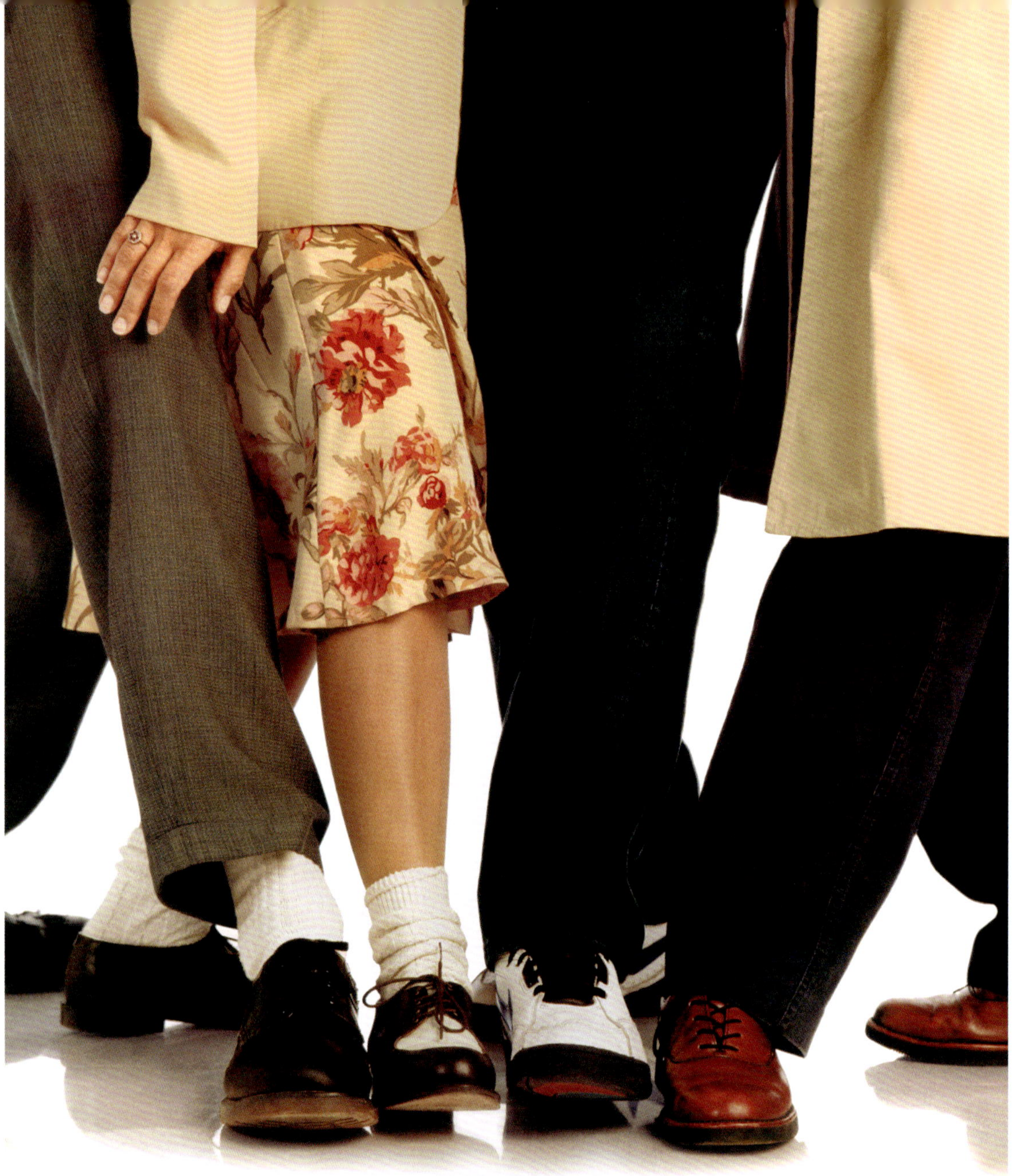

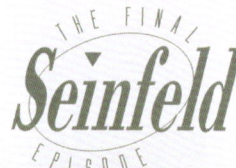

THE FINAL
Seinfeld
EPISODE

I photographed the *Seinfeld* cast several times during the height of their popularity, but I had never watched the show. I didn't watch any TV.

These actors were pros, though—it was just a matter of giving them a stage to play on. As a photographer, you need to know when to sit back and let them do their thing. Michael Richards walked pigeons on a leash (no pigeons were hurt). Jerry held his team close. They were all game to try anything. Climb up on a taxi. Hide under pigeon-shit umbrellas.

My favorite shot of the cast was taken for an ad for their last show. They were so embedded in pop culture at the time that just showing their shoes was enough for everyone to recognize them. Everyone but me, that is.

Sometimes capturing a person's humanity is as simple as letting a little light in. I had no clue what it would be like to photograph Anita Hill in 1992. After being portrayed as so one-dimensional at the Clarence Thomas hearings the year before, I needed to show her beauty and dignity.

We set up in a nondescript garage. Instead of using lights, I lifted the garage door and used the sunlight, which came pouring in to backlight her. This is one of my favorite photographs ever.

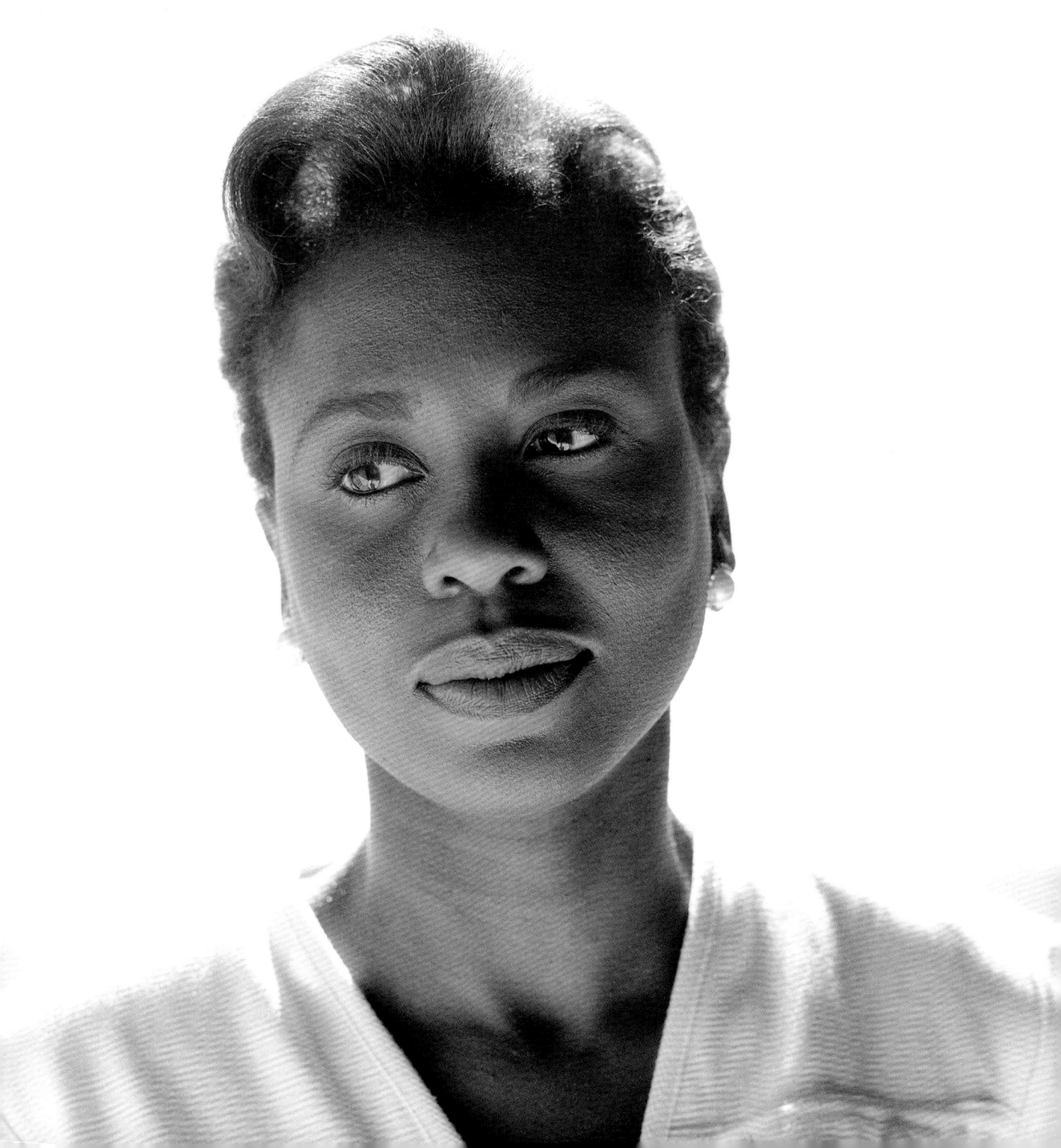

The sky above the orchards outside Cape Town were a spectacular rich blue I had never seen before. I asked four apple pickers to climb up onto their truck and throw apples up into the heavens. IBM was trying to illustrate the technology they provided to get the apples to market in Italy.

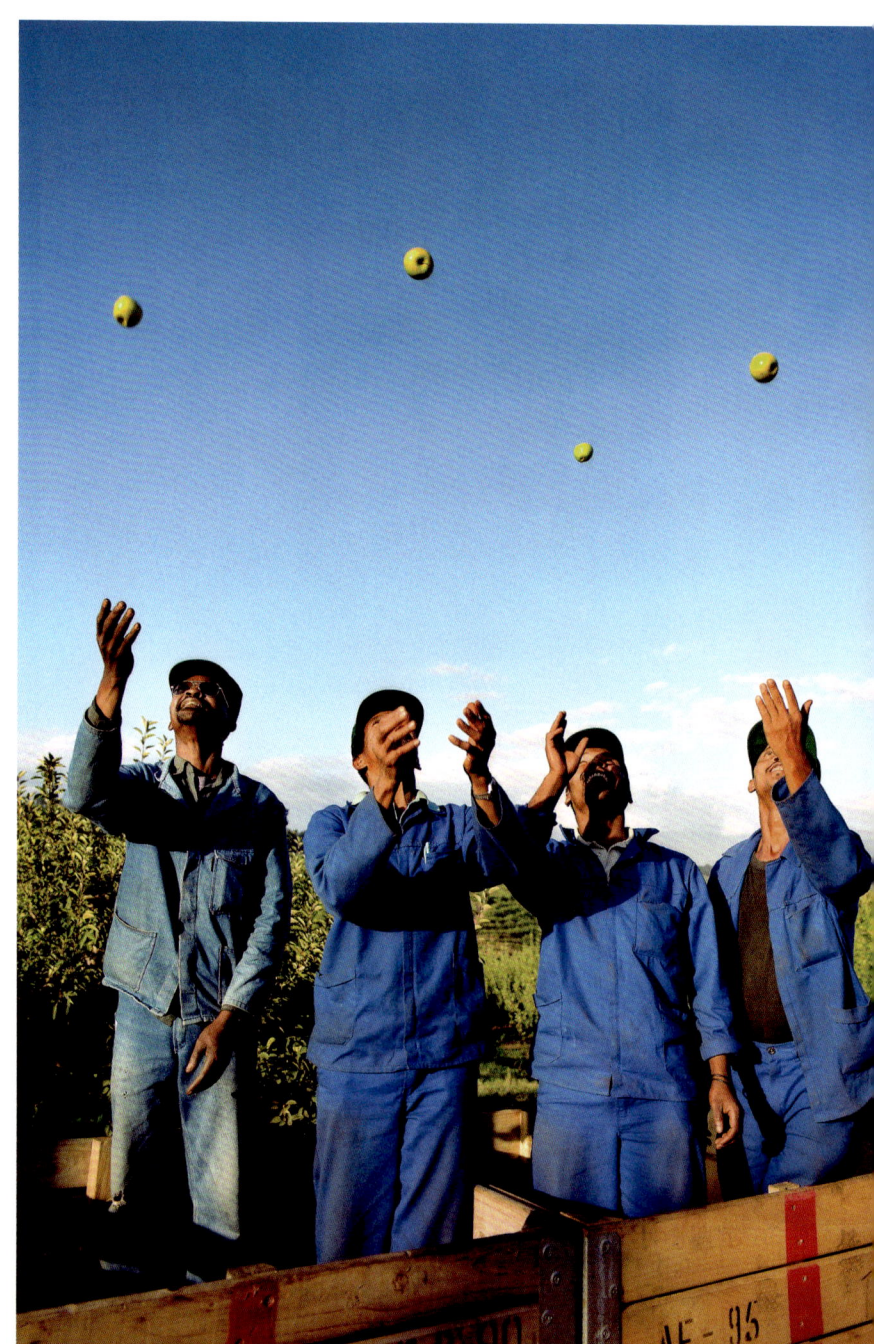

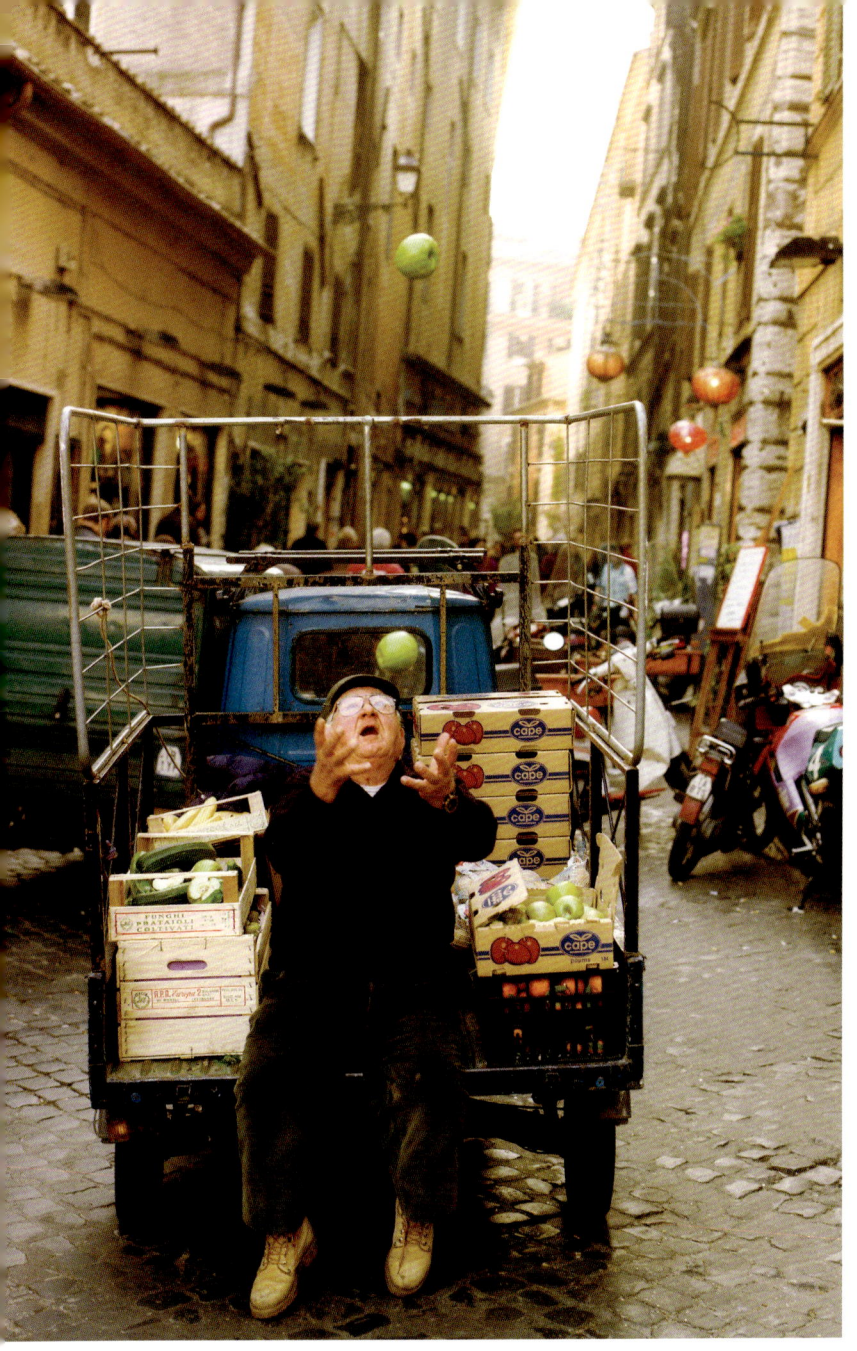

I then flew to Rome and asked the old man who ran the Campo de' Fiori market to catch the apples as they came down. I love how this series shows the different ways the world is connected, both seen and imagined.

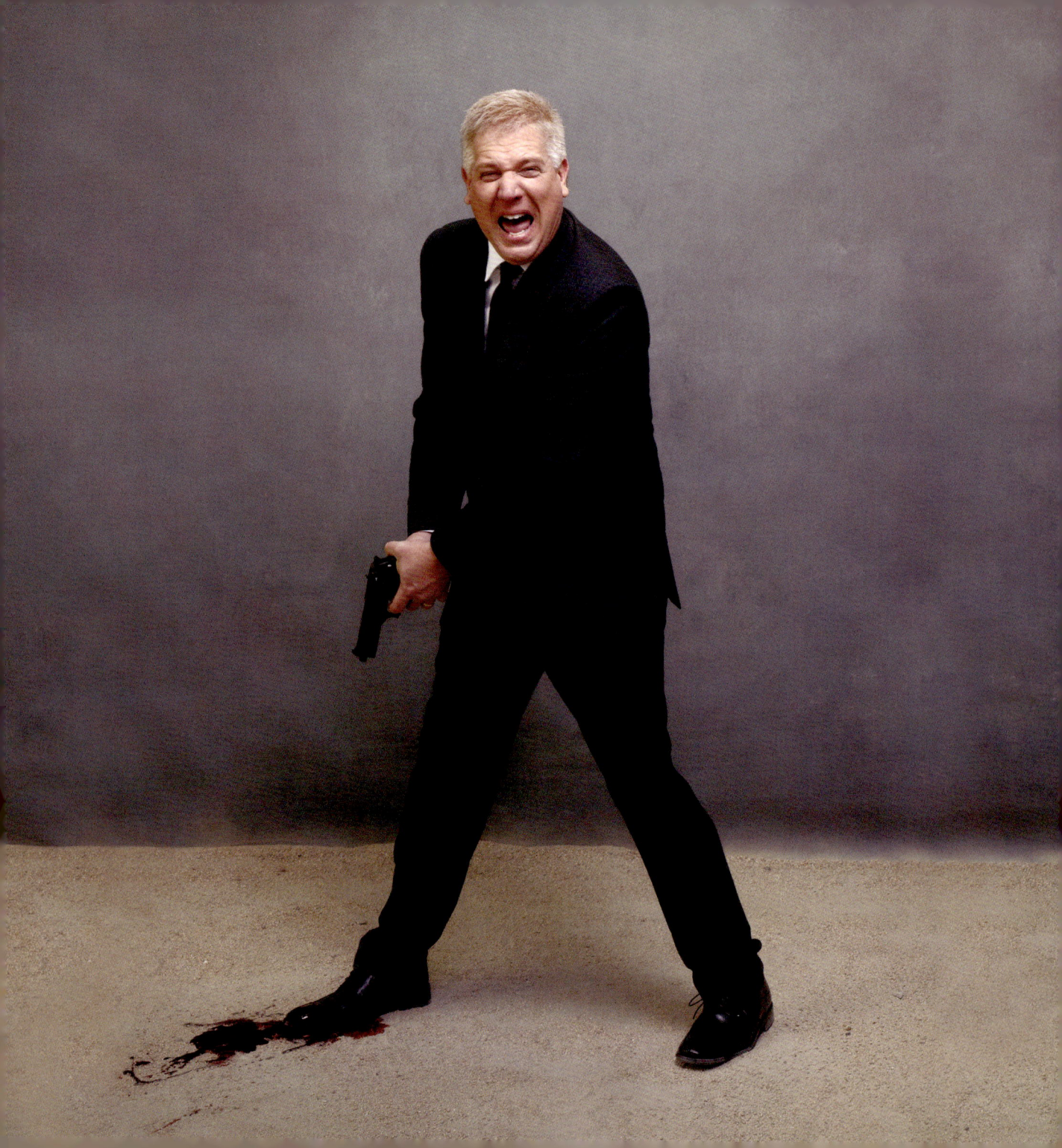

Sometimes connections aren't obvious. Glenn Beck, one of the loudest voices at Fox News, became really popular. We were thrown together by an assignment, and even though we were so far apart politically, he and I found a creative place to meet that was rich and produced some of my best images.

Glenn was fearless creatively and would take my ideas and run with them. He told me, "Anything you can dream up I will do"—and he meant it.

One time he went on air and said that Barack Obama was a racist. I immediately called him up. "That is the craziest thing I have ever heard," I said. "You just shot yourself in the foot." Next time I saw him, I took him out in the desert, drilled a hole in his shoe, had fake blood coming out of it, and I gave him a gun.

We were not trying to change each other's minds. We both just appreciated that we could meet in the middle and create something special together.

There is something so powerful about two musicians from different generations and genres comparing notes. For a story around this theme, we picked up Paul Simon in a limousine and drove out to meet with LL Cool J in Queens. LL was living in his grandmother's basement. We got there and walked past the vinyl-covered furniture in the living room and down to LL's bedroom.

At the time, Paul was working on *Graceland*, his head deep into African music. LL was really into doo-wop, where Paul cut his teeth. So, LL was trying to explain his love of doo-wop to Paul by playing his favorites. Meanwhile, Paul was sharing his love of African music. The whole time LL's grandmother was yelling down the steps, "Turn it down, Turn it down!"

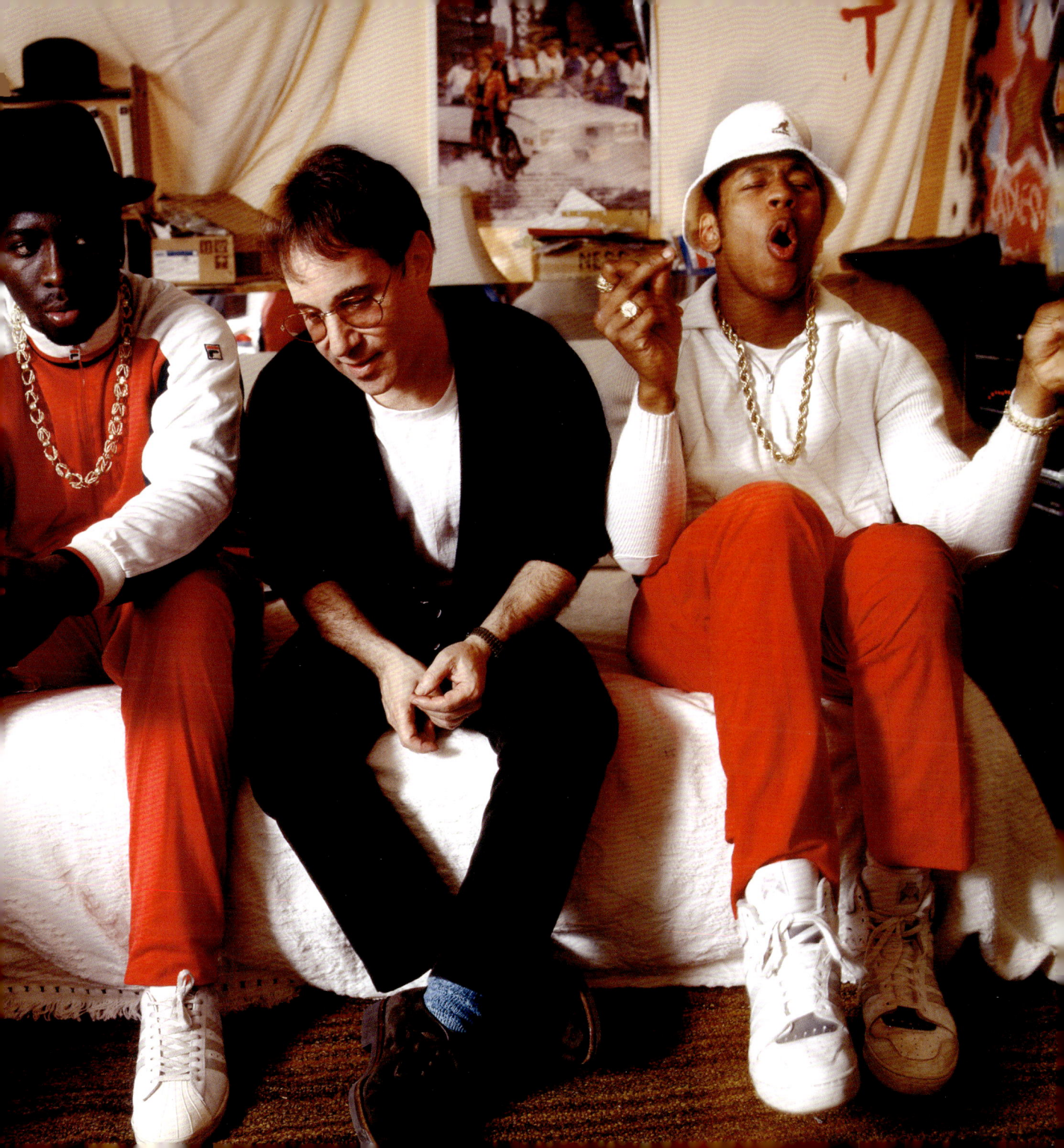

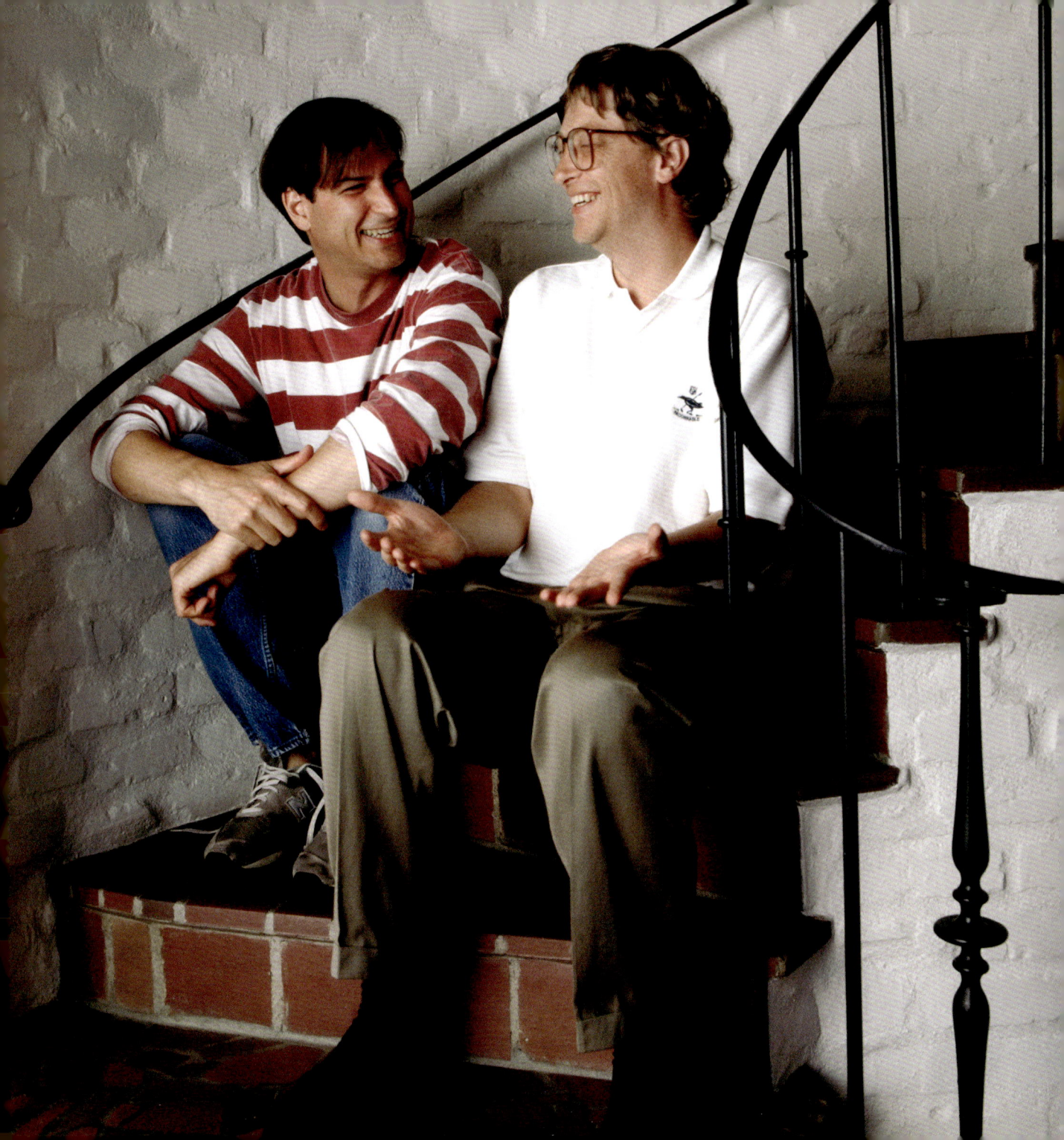

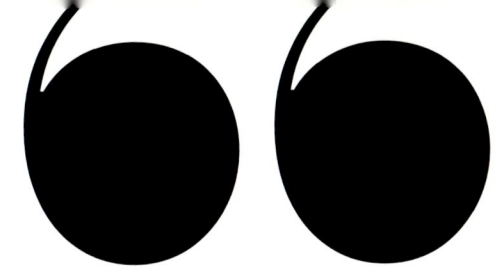

There are times when what I capture doesn't tell the whole story. While this 1991 photo of Steve Jobs and Bill Gates might be the only posed one of them together, it doesn't show what was actually going on.

At one point, they were whispering verbal jabs to each other. "You will never beat me at anything," Bill Gates said under his breath to Jobs.

Then he adjusted it a bit, "You may tie me, but you will never beat me."

I was glad to capture this moment of levity, where these two rivals were finding joy with the competition.

You may tie me, but you will never beat me.

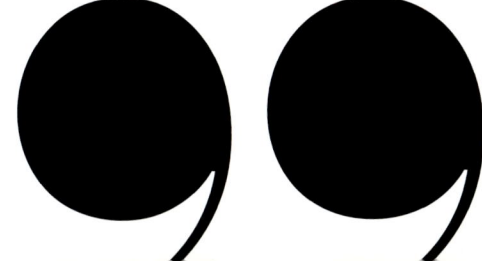

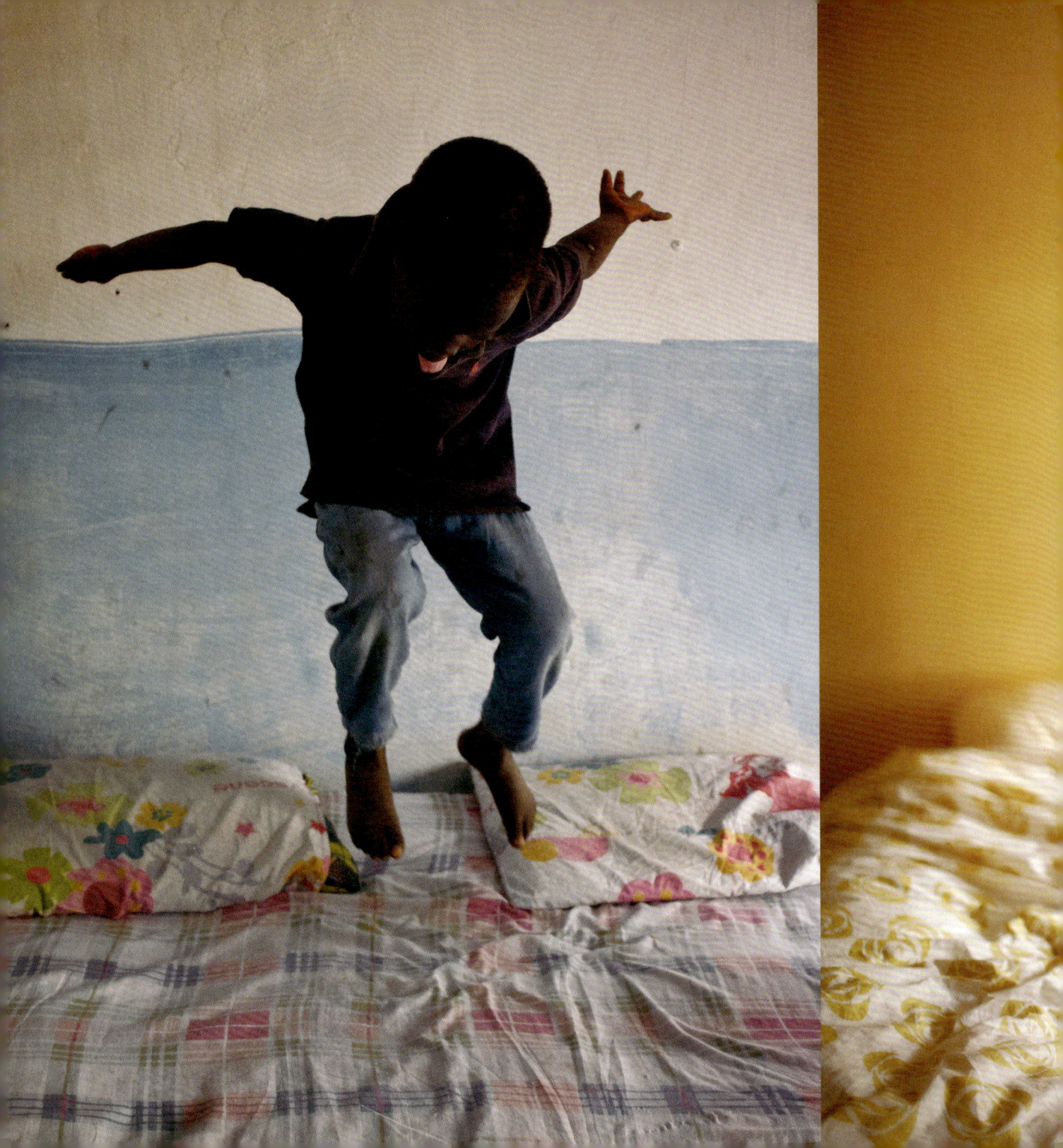

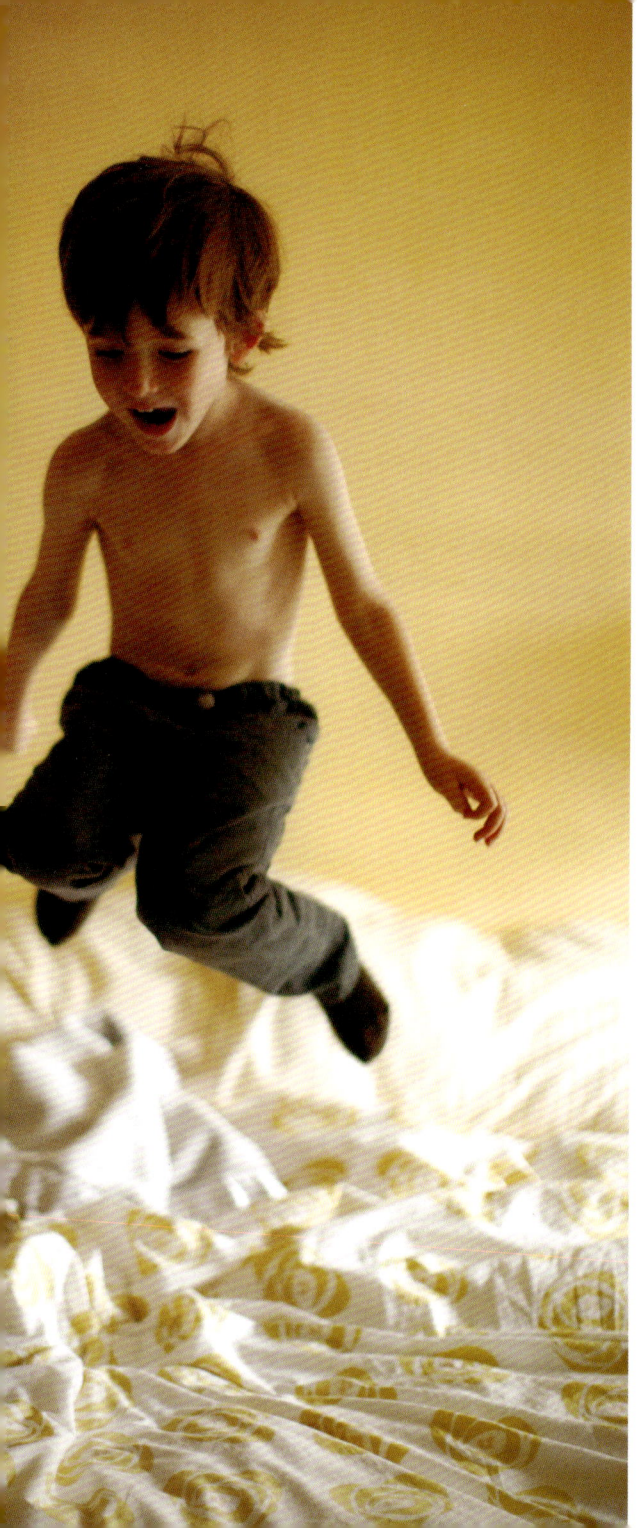

Harry Dwinell received my first book, *The Unforgettable Photograph*, for graduation from college. He signed up for the Peace Corps and took it with him when he got stationed in the small village of Panchang in The Gambia.

That's when he started a project he called "Contrasts." His photos are all re-creations of the photos in my book—the setup, the body language—with a totally new cast and location. The most intimate details are reimagined. After working on the project for months, he posted some on Facebook and tagged me. They all moved me to tears. Harry wrote that he. . . "seeks to show viewers that no matter where we live in the world, no matter our culture or back-ground, we are all humans living lives that have more in common than some might be willing to believe."

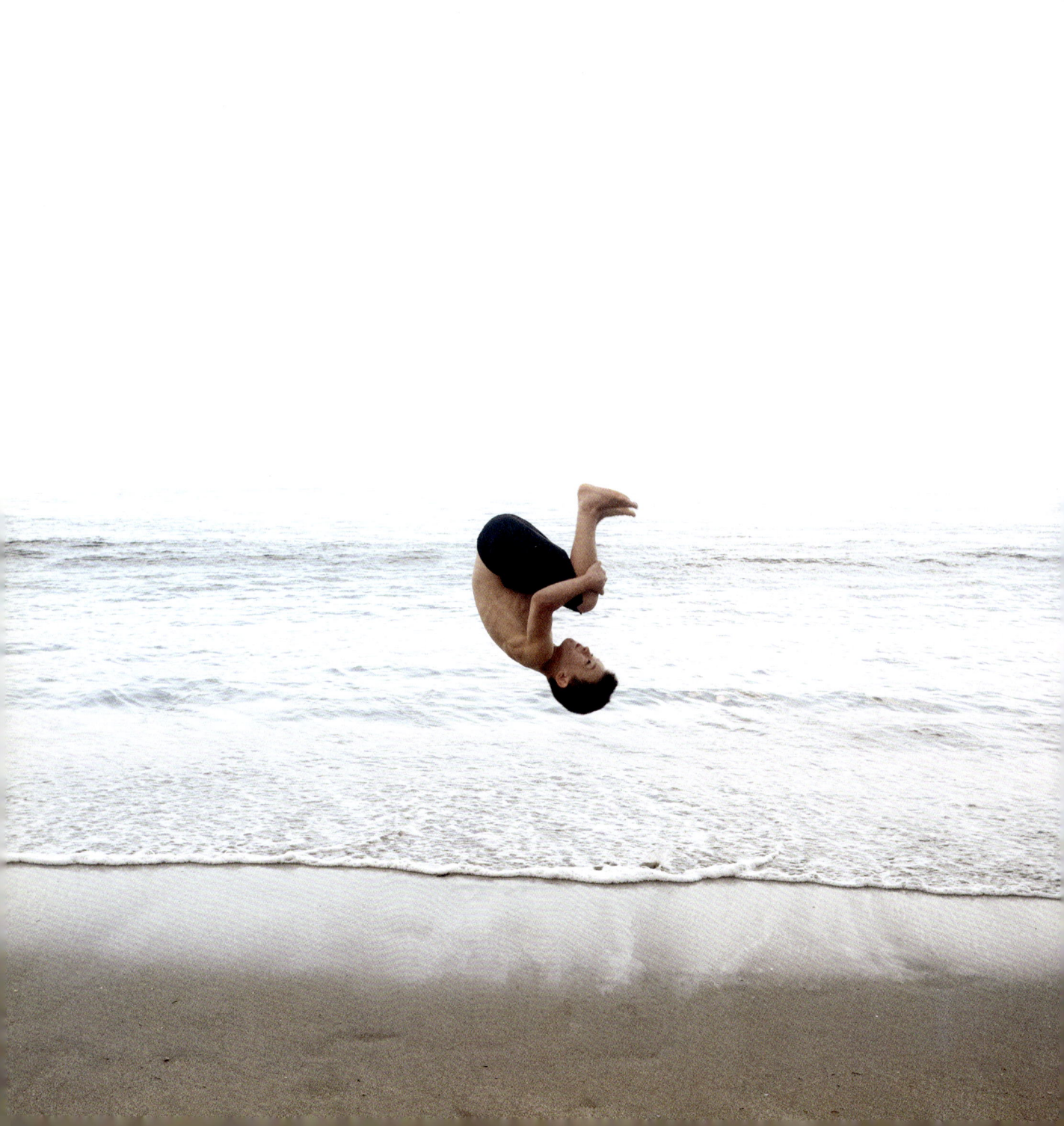

One night at dinner, I asked my kids how I stacked up in terms of hipness compared to most dads. Asher gave me a 7.5 out of 10.

"Only 7.5?" I replied.

"Dad, that is for personal style." That seemed about right.

He went on. "For knowing stuff you rate much higher!" Asher said I was at my life's peak. He then asked me to bend my head down so he could fix his hair in the reflection of my bald head.

The role of a photographer is only to be hip enough to get in the room but not have to be the center of it. I never want to be the subject. My whole approach is creating a space for people to reveal a part of themselves to me. In some ways, I am their mirror; other ways, their visual megaphone, capturing and sharing something special that gets to last forever.

But before I pick up my camera, I always pause. Even after all these years, I still don't know how the shoot will unfold, so I set my intention. It is always the same one—to find a way to put love out in the world. While it is corny to admit and hard to say out loud, I always do. And it's also my intention with these pages. I hope you feel it.

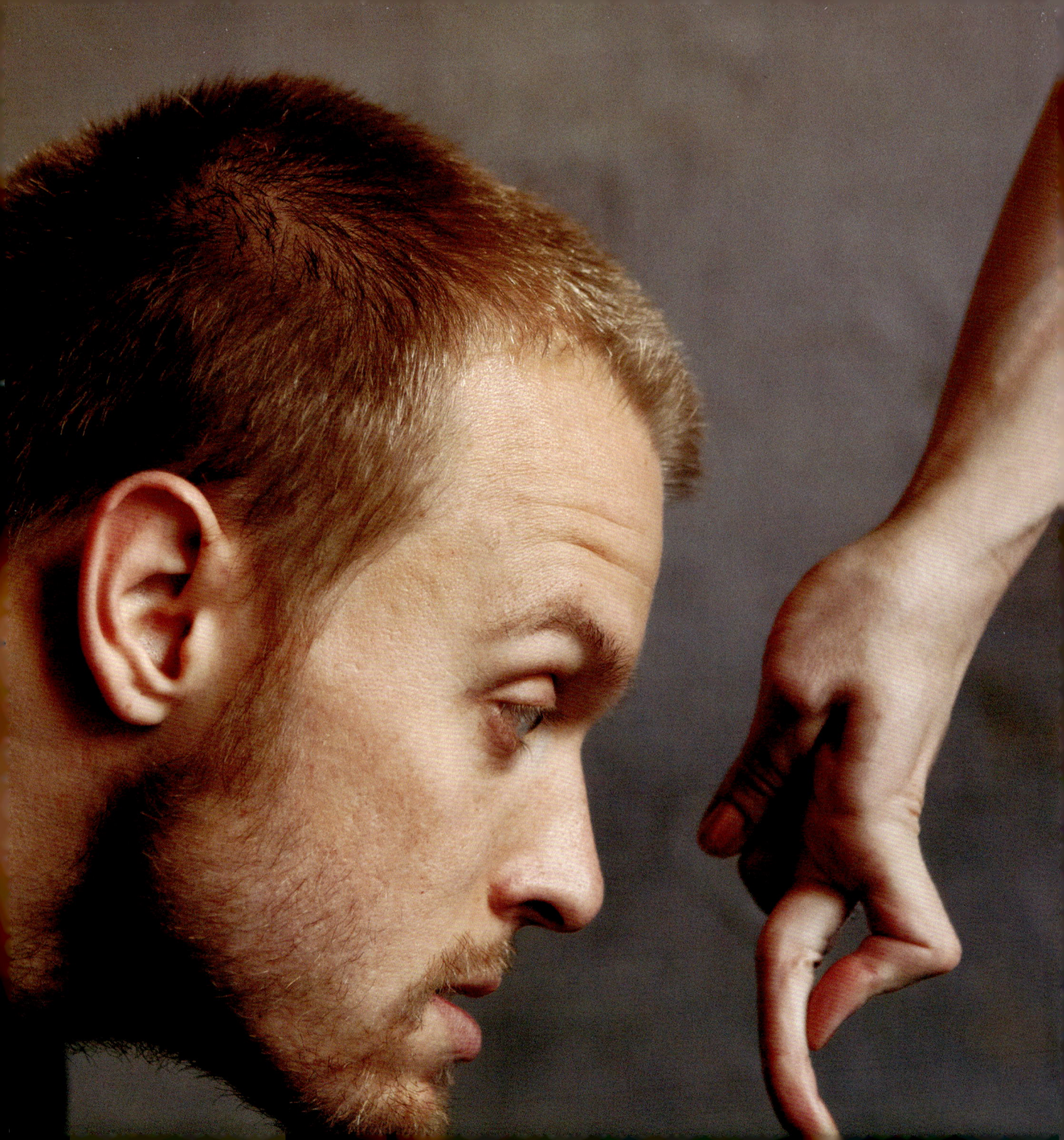

ACKNOWLEDGMENTS

This book grew out of a very happy childhood in Pittsburgh. I didn't know what that meant until I left after high school and boomeranged back several years ago. Reconnecting with my hometown allowed me also to reconnect with a very specific feeling of joy I had as a child growing up. It was a feeling of joy I subconsciously tried to recreate with all the people I photographed—and really with everything I did. Seeing that search for joy running through all of my photographs was a wild revelation. This book captures it between its covers.

It is about finding the joy that is sitting right on the end of our noses. It is both about holding onto the joy in our lives every day and appreciating the joy that is inside everyone we love.

This book was born in my mentor and friend Duane Michals's studio. When he showed me the many wonderful photo books he had created, I got jealous and wanted to make one of my own.

Pulling together *Picturing Joy* has made me grateful for all of the wonderful people who fill my life. I want to thank my hometown of Pittsburgh for being so generous and loving; my oldest and newest Pittsburgh friends—Muzz Meyers, Bob Feldman, Craig Marcus, Charlie Humphrey, Scott Baker, Eric McKenna, and Paul Rosenblatt; Sharon Dilworth, who helped me craft stories in her backyard during the COVID-19 pandemic; my New York friends Kay Unger and David Rubin, who have sheltered me with style; Kat Lam, whose support is always there; Julie Goetz from the PSO, who took the photo on page 67; and Barb Griffin, who is the most fun friend and a great person to answer the question, "Am I crazy?" Thanks also to my mother-in-law, Janet Cook, who definitely thinks I *am* crazy, and my brother Andrew who likely has similar thoughts.

I appreciate all the people who helped make this book a reality, especially Becky Randall and Nicole Gallagher at my studio; Dinah Dunn and Andrea Duarte from Indelible Editions; and everyone at Flashpoint Books.

I also couldn't have done this book without everyone who contributed to the book's Kickstarter campaign—over two hundred people and every single dollar is appreciated. Special thanks to Sherri Leopard, Jill Pearlman, Heidi Pearlman, Alan Nelson, Janet Markel, Bear Brandegee, and Nir Kossovsky. Asking for money and monetizing my creative process has never been easy for me. The support I received is both humbling and validating, as it enabled and encouraged me to bring this book out into the world. The love shared during our Kickstarter campaign as we reached our goal taught me a lot about asking for help.

Thanks also to all the people who have hired me, posed for me, shaped me, and opened doors for me to come in and take pictures. My work is inspired every day by the incredible people who trust their images to my camera.

I am very lucky. Every morning, I get to love the people closest to me before I even open my eyes. I tell Jackson and Asher how much I love being their daddy every single day—and I mean it. At the end of each day, when we stop laughing before going to sleep, I kiss Stephie, and I mean that, too. Appreciating their love is the real gift. That is what all of my photographs are created from—that love.

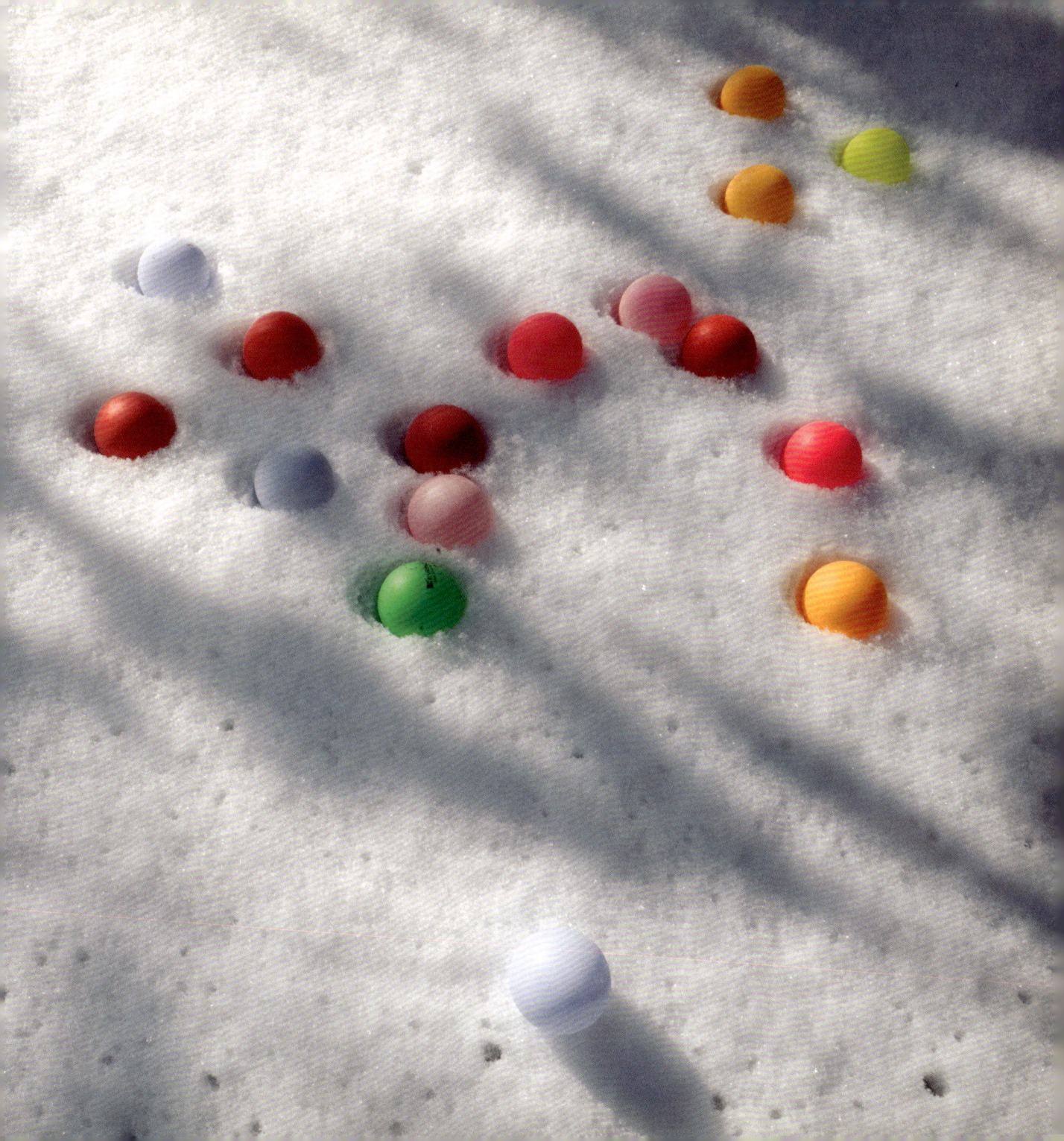

ABOUT THE AUTHOR

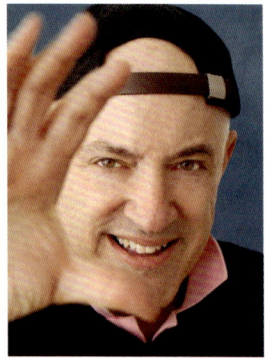

As a seven-year-old Pittsburgh kid, George Lange began snapping photos, exploring the world, and asking tons of questions. After graduating from the Rhode Island School of Design, George worked for Duane Michals and Annie Leibovitz before establishing his own career. His work has appeared in *Vogue*, *Rolling Stone*, *Vanity Fair*, *Esquire*, *People*, and the *New York Times*, among other publications. He shot many of the iconic images from TV shows such as *Friends*, *Frasier*, *Dawson's Creek*, and *Seinfeld*, as well as ads for TLC hit shows including *Cake Boss* and *Here Comes Honey Boo Boo*, and corporate clients including Dick's Sporting Goods, Twilio, and the Pittsburgh Symphony Orchestra. George's first book, *The Unforgettable Photograph: 228 Ideas, Tips, and Secrets for Taking the Best Pictures of Your Life*, sold more than fifty thousand copies and spawned multiple foreign-language editions. He recently moved back to Pittsburgh and lives in his childhood home with his wife and their two sons.

Picturing Joy is an experience that George Lange brings to life for corporate events, fundraisers, and team-building sessions. The events include talks that share George's enthusiasm and joy with stories from his career, workshops with inside tips for capturing images in new ways, and commercial and private photo sessions.

Contact George's studio for further details: studio@langestudio.com, or visit **georgelange.com**.